WORK
JERKS

WORK JERKS

JERKS

How to
Cope with <u>Difficult</u>
Bosses and Colleagues

Louise Carnachan

SHE WRITES PRESS

Published 2022
Printed in the United States of America
Print ISBN: 978-1-64742-369-8
E-ISBN: 978-1-64742-370-4
Library of Congress Control Number: 2021924755

For information, address:
She Writes Press
1569 Solano Ave #546
Berkeley, CA 94707

Interior design by Tabitha Lahr

She Writes Press is a division of SparkPoint Studio, LLC.

To the wonderful people I have met in my career
and from whom I have learned so much. Thank you!

CONTENTS

PREFACE

ean-Paul Sartre said, "Hell is other people." You may
agree. Being in any community requires tolerance,
patience, and the willingness to give people a pass—even
if it's more often than you'd like. The definition of a "jerk"
is in the eye of the beholder. People do things that push our
individual buttons but don't bother others. Yet some behaviors annoy almost everyone. We've all worked with jerks,
and *we've all been jerks*. I'm guessing you selected this book
because you have a colleague who's really on your nerves.
Your nemesis could be your special problem or may have a
reputation for being a pill with everyone. And if a copy of
this book was anonymously left on your desk? Well, then . . .

If you find yourself fuming, getting sick, complaining
incessantly to friends and family (who are tired of hearing
about it), lying awake at night, and/or dreading going to
work, it's time for a change. *There's help in these pages!*

It's impossible to foresee how the world of work will
morph over time, but what will endure is the quirkiness of
people. Irritating coworkers will find a way to reveal their
stripes whether in person, via email, text, Zoom, Slack or the
next virtual platform in the wings. This book is designed to
provide you with practical ideas that can be adapted to any

medium. It provides options of what to do, above and beyond what you've already tried. You may be pleasantly surprised that little tweaks can make a big difference.

Doing something to improve your situation is powerful; you stop being a victim, might get a better night's sleep, have happier days at work, and, just maybe, develop an improved relationship with your work jerk. And if you discover you've been the problem? There's help for that too. Ready to do something to make things better? Good, let's get started!

Chapter One:

HOW TO USE THIS BOOK

Up front you need to know there's no way you're going to make your problem coworker change. That's an inside job for that person. What you have control over is what you think (which feeds how you feel) and what you do. That's where we'll focus: how to change the situation by changing what you think, say, and do.

I expect you to use judgment as you evaluate these ideas. Don't do things you're pretty sure will get you fired (unless that's your goal!). But don't discard suggestions out of hand either. Consider this a shoe-shopping expedition: try things on, walk around a bit, then make up your mind about what you want to keep or discard.

I know firsthand what it's like to be furious, hurt, baffled, or dumbfounded by someone's workplace behavior. Earlier in my career, I was certain it was personal. Over the years I've learned that's rarely the case. People act the way they do because it works for them, they don't know how to do anything differently, or it's the best they can do with the resources they have. You may have noticed that other people can be with your problem person and witness the very same things you see yet don't come away from the interaction feeling the way you do.

We all have filters to make meaning of our environment. Our first set of filters came from the circumstances in which we were born (i.e., race, gender, class, region, etc.). Other important filters came from our families or caretakers. These were installed very early in life and may need a good spring-cleaning, if not replacement. Part of the work of dealing with difficult people is to realize what's going on with you (what's pushing your buttons) and then decide if that's how you want to live. Only you can change your mind and act in ways that help yourself.

Who am I? I'm a white, boomer, cisgender, heterosexual woman. I've worked with, taught, and coached many people who don't share my background. For over forty years I've been in the trenches of companies as a coach, trainer, and, most importantly, as an employee. I graduated as a clinical social worker specializing in cognitive behavioral therapy and how systems affect individuals. Early on I veered away from being a therapist to teaching and advising others on teamwork, leadership, and communication. I've worked as an employee and as a consultant in a number of industries. I've coached and taught thousands of people suffering from workplace relationship issues. I've counseled both the aggrieved and those who cause the grief, managers, and team members. I've also had my own share of jerk challenges, so I know how draining it can be. What I offer draws from behavioral methods, conflict management principles, emotional intelligence theories and practice, and The School of Hard Knocks (i.e., what works in real life and in real jobs).

After decades of observing and interacting with folks at work, I've accumulated a compendium of behavior patterns I'm calling jerk archetypes, or "Jerketypes." Each Jerketype has subtypes, or variations on a theme. In the following chapters, we'll cover:

- **The Narcissist** (It's all about ME!)
- **The Know-It-All** (I have an answer—even when there's no question)
- **The Incompetent** (What, huh?)
- **The Runaway Train** (A variety of extreme behaviors)
- **The Fight-or-Flee** (Dukes up—or run)
- **The Poor Me** (Versions of victimhood and helplessness)
- **The Not-So-Funny Jokester** (Ha-ha?)
- **The We Are Family** (Relationships at work)
- **The Habitually Annoying Jerk** (A potpourri of highly irritating behaviors), and finally,
- **When the "Jerk" is a Toxic Work Culture** (The problem is larger than any one individual).

The terms used in this book are informal, although some of the words have everyday, legal, or psychiatric meanings (such as bullying, narcissists). I don't provide legal advice or psychiatric diagnoses. The colleagues and clients I've coached over the years have asked for practical ideas about what to do and haven't been very interested in how the person became a jerk to begin with. I've intentionally stayed light on the "whys" and heavy on "how-tos."

Yes, it's possible that addictions and/or disorders are influencing your person. But you can't solve those issues (or any of their issues, actually), so the focus of this book is on actions *you* can take.

Where to Start

As you look through the table of contents, choose the most obvious characteristic of your problem person. Of course, there can be overlap among Jerketypes; the Narcissist can also be a Know-It-All or a Runaway Train. An Incompetent can also be a Poor Me, a Narcissist, or even worse, a Know-It-All. The combinations are endless.

If you're not sure after looking at the table of contents, put on your detective hat. What does your difficult coworker *do* that pushes you over the edge? Be as specific and objective as you can be, as if you were a video recording. Is it the person's tone of voice? Their choice of words? Is it a physical issue, like hovering over your shoulder? Maybe they have a habit, such as consistently being late to work, or telling you what to do, or cracking poorly timed jokes. Once you have a better idea of exactly what's bugging you, look again at the table of contents, or read the beginning of each chapter, to see if you can identify similarities to your jerk. More than one type may apply.

About Jerks

Not all Jerketypes are equally destructive. There's even a spectrum within each type. Some of them you may be sympathetic to, or consider benign, although other colleagues are bothered by them. What puts folks firmly in jerk territory is engaging in *consistently annoying actions over a sustained period of time.* All of us can be problematic on a particular day or week. It's the relentlessness of their behavior that gains admission to what I call the Pest Hall of Fame.

If you like and care about someone, you probably have a longer fuse than you would with a colleague you don't like. If it's a brief encounter, or somebody you rarely see, you're likely to let it go. But if it's a coworker with whom you interact daily, and what they do is grating on your last nerve, you might want to do something. At the very least, you'll want to deal with your emotions so you can come down off the ceiling. My suggestions are designed to address ongoing, habitual frustrations with someone that you want/need to remain friendly so you can continue to work together.

If your strategy to date has been to complain to others, this release valve isn't effective in solving the problem. In fact, by whining you may have become a jerk for someone else. Letting a flood of anger out through gossip may feel better at the moment—but then the upset builds again and you're back to leaking venom. There's no lasting effect *and* you're negatively impacting others. I hope you'll decide to engage in strategies that have the possibility of producing positive change.

The Assumptions

First, I presume that you want to keep your job and improve the relationship with your difficult colleague (or at least make it tolerable). Second, I assume you're willing to take sensible action and try things out to see what works best. If you want things to shift, you're going to need to do something different—not just hope and pray that they will have a life-altering epiphany, move out of state, or find a new job. I'll provide tools; it's up to you to experiment.

My other assumptions are:

- You realize the only one you can change is you;
- You'll use good judgment about what's safe to try in your environment;
- You know (or can find out) what resources are available to you in your specific workplace, e.g., human resources, union rep, ombudsperson, legal department, etc.;
- You'll look for improvements and allow your problem person the opportunity to grow.

The last point can be tough to swallow. When we've had lousy interactions with someone, or they've hurt us, we don't necessarily see that they're behaving better because our filters have been narrowed to look for evidence that they're despicable. If we're stuck in a story of their awfulness, we don't

5

look for signs of positive change—instead we're engaged in confirmation bias, which is interpreting new evidence as verification of our existing beliefs. Be aware of that trap and make a concerted effort to notice others' progress.

Is It You?

Since we're all human, we're subject to biases. Most of these predispositions, like the filters described earlier, come from childhood. Evaluate the commonalities of people who annoy you. Do you share any of these characteristics? If it's something you don't like about yourself, that's good information. Is it a quality that reminds you of a family member? If it's a "type" that gets on your nerves, then it's easier not to take it personally. It may be your sensitivity that's getting in your way.

It's important to recognize that most people don't have big issues with others at work, most of the time. If you *always* seem to have a problem with someone, I'd invite you to take a deeper look at yourself. What you may have thought was "*They* are the matter with me," could well be "*I* am the matter with me." It's courageous to look at yourself and your contribution to relationship difficulties—work or personal. The degree to which you're suffering may say more about you than the other person, so take this opportunity to learn more about yourself. Please know I'm cheering you on in your quest for self-understanding.

A Warning

If you're in a situation that's dangerous, i.e., you feel you or others are in physical danger, or you're dealing with someone who is highly abusive, unpredictable, and/or threatening, *please pay attention to your safety* and immediately get help from your company's human resources, security, and/or community law enforcement. Don't delay!

About the Case Examples

I illustrate points through case studies. They are composites of people I've known over my long career, so they're based in reality but the specifics have been altered. People's issues may have been combined, and identifying information has been removed.

In the End . . .

What we do for a living may differ, but people are still people with all their talents and idiosyncrasies. If you feel crappy about work every day because of a jerk, I hope you'll choose action over inaction. My experience tells me there are probably things you can do to make a positive difference in your situation. I'm rooting for you!

Chapter Two:

THE NARCISSISTIC JERK

We'll start our tour with the royalty of all jerks, the Narcissistic Jerk, because the most extreme version can be devastating to your career. They're not only difficult to work with, they can leave you questioning your sanity. If you're dealing with one now, you have my condolences. To be fair, we can all have narcissistic moments. I flush with embarrassment over my own moments of self-importance, when I thought I knew more, or needed to have the attention placed on me instead of sharing. No doubt I'll have additional self-absorbed bumbles throughout the balance of my life. What makes a person fall into this jerk category is a consistent pattern of behavior over time, not the occasional lapses we all have.

There's a spectrum of narcissistic behavior at work. In this chapter we'll cover some, but not all, versions of this type:

- **The Narcissistic Leader** (No really, it *is* all about ME!)
- **The Gang Leader** (We're cool, but we hate "them.")
- **The Dramatic** (What do you mean suffer in silence?)
- **The Non-Stop Talker** (And one more thing . . .)

The Narcissistic Leader

While I paint a pretty damning picture of this type, many narcissists have enduring relationships—which seems astonishing given their traits. Those of you who fall into the category of being "nice" are particularly vulnerable to narcissists. You may tolerate what others would consider abuse and/or make excuses for them.

You'll recognize the Narcissistic Leader by the following:

- They seek power and control through directing and manipulating others.
- They lack empathy; it's their most telling characteristic. They have no idea what it's like for someone else. You might think they empathize with you (or with the people closest to them), but that's just because they have sloppy boundaries. If you're part of the inner circle, in their mind you've become part of them.
- They demand a loyalty that is not mutual. They carefully distribute praise and affection on an inner circle to suck in followers. At some point supporters are kicked to the curb.
- They share information with you that they swear no one else knows in order to make you feel special. Later, you find out a number of others have been privy to these "secrets."
- They're not very sympathetic. If you can't get an assignment to them when they want it (never mind you just had brain surgery and are still in the hospital), you've disappointed them and held them up.
- They can find your weak points and manipulate them just as readily as they find your strong points and get you to do their work. For example, if you seem vulnerable to flattery, they'll shamelessly cajole you into putting together a document that is their work to do.

- They will lie mercilessly to get what they want. The generous take is that they're not even aware it's a lie. Their internal dialogue must involve convincing themselves they're right, they deserve it, or other people are idiots or are out to get them. When you know the facts or truth, their lies can be crazymaking.

Narcissistic Leaders are particularly dangerous when they're also charismatic and intelligent. They often rise to leadership positions because they play politics (both capital P and lowercase p) extremely well. Since they've managed to climb the ladder so far (or move to a different ladder), there's no reason for them to believe they can't continue. Make no mistake, they're out for themselves. Often coworkers don't believe, or recognize, the depth of the narcissist's self-absorption; it's all-consuming.

To be clear, you need self-confidence to lead—which isn't to be confused with narcissism. True leaders don't manipulate people for their own aims. Instead, they have healthy egos fed by self-esteem. They're not prone to lying or believing inaccurate perceptions of the world around them—or their exalted place in it. True leaders have the confidence to ask for feedback, recognize their foibles, and learn from them. Narcissistic Leaders barrel through life with blinders on, and with little interest in changing their ways, regardless of how many people they harm along the way.

Some of us have special antennae for this Jerketype because we grew up watching narcissists in their natural habitat (i.e., our families or people in our immediate environment). Others of us are more likely to be taken in because we want to believe the best of the person, or we find ways to justify their behavior. Some people are so shocked anyone would behave this way, they don't know what to do and let it go—sometimes repeatedly.

Morgan, the Narcissistic Leader, and
His Merry Band of Minions

Morgan took an executive position with the company after leaving his previous job as a high-level sales director. A few weeks into his tenure, I attended his presentation to a large group of employees. The way in which Morgan engaged his audience gave me pause. He worked the room, telling a personal story with a crack in his voice and a tear in his eye. He manipulated this group to pony up monetary donations that in the end would make *him* look good. Afterward, people told me they thought he was a great hire, such a wonderful presenter, and an asset to the organization. My internal alarms were ringing.

Fast-forward eighteen months. Morgan worked his way to the top of his reporting line by undercutting his incompetent (and subsequently fired) boss. One of Morgan's managers, Gabe, came to me to discuss his concerns about the department now that Morgan had taken the reins. Gabe wondered if he was being negative, or whether he actually had cause for worry. He started with the great quote from Joseph Heller's *Catch-22*, "Just because you're paranoid doesn't mean they aren't after you."

Gabe's story began with Morgan firing a clutch of good, stable, tenured workers and replacing them with a set of lesser-talented Morgan-supporters. This crew was comprised of three administrative gossips and a clueless manager. Due to alleged time constraints, Morgan declined to meet with the few direct reports who remained from the old crowd; Gabe was one. However, Morgan seemed to have plenty of time for luncheons and happy hours with his new golden people.

Gabe reported that things took a turn from bad to horrid when a whispering campaign began regarding two of the department's highest achievers, one of whom was a friend of his. The most despicable action involved Morgan directing his minions to look for and document "evidence" to destroy this person's credibility and question their competence. I'd seen some appalling behavior over the years, but this was pure malice on Morgan's part. Gabe had been approached to participate in this enterprise, which he managed to sidestep.

Gabe asked if I thought he was reading things into Morgan's actions, and maybe it wasn't as bad as he thought? I couldn't reassure him; it seemed to me that he'd read the situation accurately. I suggested he continue to stay "under the radar" and asked if he had a plan B in the event he became the next victim.

In the end, Gabe survived, and Morgan didn't. Sadly, his termination wasn't for his actions with his staff but instead for publicly embarrassing the company by making statements to the media that weren't his to make. His replacement put Morgan's Minions on performance improvement plans. None of them succeeded—to the surprise of no one.

You might wonder why Morgan would get rid of the people who were actually doing the work and made the department (and ultimately him) look good. They were too much of a threat. Instead of supporting his staff members, he worried about who might gain favor with senior executives. He assumed that anyone who had a positive reputation would make him look bad by contrast. Morgan's game plan: clean house of the competent, flatter the flunkies, then shake his head woefully, professing to his boss that he couldn't get traction because he'd had so much turnover. Meanwhile, he collected a hefty paycheck by playing his sleight-of-hand shell game.

How to Deal with a Narcissistic Leader

I've seen a number of narcissists in my life and career. They can be charming—for a while, particularly if you aren't close to them. But if they're making your work life miserable, try the following:

- Stay out of the inner sanctum (the favored group). If you're unduly flattered by them, see it for what it is. Keeping some distance may lead you to feel marginalized, and you probably won't be treated as warmly as a result. Understand that those who are currently the chosen are one sword stroke away from being decapitated.
- Find excuses to avoid off-site social events if invited by the narcissist. If you relent, go infrequently and make sure you aren't the last one there—or there by yourself.
- *Do not* share personal information that's important to you; it's likely to come back to haunt you. And don't share gossip or speculation about others. Become a master of sharing a few inconsequential facts or opinions without getting in very deep. It's a fine line between being friendly and being in the inner circle.
- Don't solicit personal information from this type of leader. If it's offered, remain at the most superficial level, such as "Sorry to hear that," then change the subject back to the work at hand.
- If you get a promotion because of this person, they'll extract a price—if not now, then later. Know that if you become a threat because of your expertise or political standing, they'll attempt to take you down by eroding your image. Unless you're protected by someone they can't sway, start looking for your next position away from their influence.
- Do a realistic assessment about where both of you are in your careers and what this leader's pattern of changing jobs has been. You might be able to outlast this jerk.
- Assume they're there to stay if this person was protected and promoted by someone at the top. Plan accordingly.

- Get the directives and expectations in writing if you're asked to do an assignment that you feel puts you at risk. An answer from them in response to an email you've written about your understanding of the task may be enough to provide you with documentation if you need it.
- Seek a reporting mechanism if what they're doing is unethical or illegal; either go through human resources or a whistleblower hotline if you have one.
- Consider your alternatives, decide what you want to do, then act. Only you can figure out how to make a living wage and not lose your sanity at the same time. What isn't helpful is to whine and stew. Even if you aren't ecstatic about the options, carefully examine what you *can* do. It may be that you need to leave for a new opportunity.

WORKSHEET:

IF YOU THINK YOU MAY BE A NARCISSISTIC LEADER

If you've read this far, perhaps you don't feel good about some of the things you've done. Maybe you're starting to wonder if you should make some changes in your beliefs and actions. I highly recommend that you seek a counselor or therapist to help you find tools and provide support.

Please answer the following questions with a yes or no. For each yes answer, see the advice that follows the question.

1. Do you believe you've earned all the good you've got?

A lack of humility is not only an unattractive trait, it's indicative of a lack of awareness of how others have helped you, and to what degree you've benefitted from circumstances. People notice when they're stepped over or stepped on. Make a point of thanking people publicly for the things they've done.

2. Do you stretch the truth to get what you need or want? Do you tell people what they want to hear to gain their cooperation?

Lying can come back to haunt you and tank your career. If people find out they've been manipulated, they'll likely distance themselves, spread word of your misdeeds, and maybe even try to get you fired. If you're engaged in unethical or illegal practices, you run the risk of extremely serious consequences above and beyond job termination. If lying or manipulation have become habits, you might want to seek counseling. Your relationships could benefit from it.

3. Do you have a need to be in control and become anxious if you aren't? Do you make decisions that affect others without gaining their support?

Controlling others is a problem for both work and nonwork relationships. You might benefit from counseling on this issue. Yes, sometimes leaders have to make decisions on their own, but not in every situation. Because you rely on others to carry out directives, it's best if they have some ownership. They might have good ideas too. Ask others for their point of view or how they would improve a decision. Listen carefully, include their options when you can, and thank contributors. If you fail to involve others, and they disagree with your directives over time, you're likely to lose their support.

4. Have you been told you're self-centered, arrogant, or egotistical and lack interest in other people's concerns?

Examine the behaviors that you engage in that make you appear to be self-centered. It's quite possible they indicate a lack of expressed empathy (being able to see things from another person's point of view and communicate that). If multiple people have given you this feedback, I'd suggest you check in with a counselor.

5. Do your closest allies depend upon you for their status and do whatever you ask? Do you demand loyalty in return? Are you constantly strategizing about who is loyal and who is not?

There's a lot wrong with these situations, not the least of which may be having people follow you without question into sketchy business practices. If people are afraid of your reaction, you can be kept from vital information, and that's risky to all of you. Leadership by political intrigue means that you need to be constantly vigilant regarding who's on what side, who deserves reward, and who must be punished. If you're interested in abandoning this practice, seek a coach or counselor.

6. If people disappoint you or put you in a bad light, do you make sure they pay?

Screwing up other people's careers because you're unhappy isn't okay. This signals emotionally immature behavior and a lack of ability to deal with uncomfortable feelings.

<><><><><><><><><><><><><><><><><><><><><><><><><><><><><><><><><><><><><><><><>

The Gang Leader

Like the Narcissistic Leader, these people have the self-centeredness and charisma to be dangerous. Although they're not in any formal leadership position, don't underestimate their ability to gather a following. As "informal" leaders, or influencers, they can split a well-functioning team into factions. *Please note: not all informal leaders are narcissists.*

You'll recognize the Gang Leader by their strategies, which may include:

- Questioning the authority and the skill of leadership—publicly and/or behind their backs. They're a nightmare to manage because they always know how it should be done better. They sow seeds of discontent within the staff so that they, too, question the leader's competence. Sometimes they have just enough information that the manager is left feeling insecure in their own authority.
- Creating a gang within the team (also known as a clique) that shuns or acts badly toward others in the department. It can start out innocently enough, with a group that likes to eat lunch or take breaks together, then transform into the "in-crowd" and the "out-crowd." If this reminds you of the school cafeteria, you'd be correct.
- Identifying weaknesses in others to manipulate them socially, as well as getting others to do their work.
- Criticizing with no positive suggestions for change. They have ideas about what other people should do, never what *they* could do to make things better.
- Recruiting of gang members. If they don't have a following, they hold little sway and tend to be Know-It-All's (see the next chapter) or gossips.
- Taking their complaints to someone higher up than their own manager. Jumping up the chain of command accelerates if their supervisor gives them critical feedback.
- Forming alliances and enemies—just like the Narcissistic Leader does. They have an ability to switch on a dime depending on who will give them what they want.
- Saying hurtful things with little or no remorse. They feel entitled to be mean because they lack empathy.

Samantha and Her Coven

Samantha came to the organization as a skilled technician. She got good reviews from her patients, but she was an absolute misery for her manager, Ashley, because of her sarcastic and critical comments about management.

Samantha demonstrated her charisma by telling funny family stories and garnered quite a following among the staff. Soon a group of four or five joined Samantha for lunch every day in the breakroom. The conversation would turn to talking about other staff: who they didn't like, who they thought was incompetent, and, of course, complaints about management. If one of the maligned walked into the breakroom, a hush fell. People aren't stupid—they know when they are being talked about.

Ashley perked up her ears when she noticed whispered vitriol among staff at the computer kiosks. Samantha was the constant; ever-present for gossip sessions. Ashley called Samantha into her office to have a chat about her expectations regarding teamwork and respect for all workers.

Samantha came in armed with examples of others' poor performance. Ashley redirected the conversation back to the expectations she had for Samantha's behavior. However, Ashley noted to herself that Samantha was accurate about performance issues in the department.

When a lead position in their area came up, Samantha applied for it. In terms of technical expertise, she was the most qualified. Ashley, ignoring her fear that Samantha didn't have the emotional maturity for the job, gave her the promotion anyway. Things went downhill from there.

Samantha ruled her gang with an iron fist. If anyone was friendly to the out-crowd, they were shunned for a time. She was "too busy" with her lead tasks to do the other parts of her job; her cronies were expected to step up and do her work. Favoritism was evident in shift and duty assignments. Ashley kept intervening to correct injustices and give feedback to

Samantha—which Samantha brushed off. By now Ashley had a serious morale problem in the department and came to my door begging for help.

When we spoke, Ashely admitted that Samantha had been a lousy choice for promotion. The misgivings she'd had about Samantha's interactions with team members were valid, and Ashley regretted that she hadn't paid attention to her instincts. We created a performance improvement plan (PIP) for Samantha to specify what she needed to demonstrate to be a better communicator and lead. Then we talked about how to monitor the plan closely for improvements, or lack thereof. We looped in the human resources representative in case Samantha wasn't able to turn things around in the time frame she was given. Termination would be the next step if she couldn't make the required improvements.

A PIP is no fun for anyone. The manager ends up spending an inordinate amount of time on one employee, and that person hates being watched. Two weeks into the PIP, Ashely told me she knew Samantha was looking for another job because Samantha was calling in sick a lot—and her wardrobe had suddenly spiffed up.

Within four weeks Samantha had accepted a position at another company as a lead, of course, because she now had that title on her résumé. Lesson learned, Ashely appointed a new lead from her existing staff who had excellent interpersonal skills and good technical skills.

How to Deal with a Gang Leader: Advice for Coworkers

When faced with a Gang Leader, either because they're trying to recruit you or because you've become the object of their venom, you might try the following:

- Call it like you see it. The Gang Leader, like the bully, gets much of their power from operating in a shadow world. People are too nice or too intimidated to say, "I see what you're doing—stop it." To paraphrase words from the "What If They Use Dirty Tricks?" section of the classic *Getting to Yes* by Roger Fisher and William Ury: "If I didn't know better, I'd say you were (fill in the blank of what you see or hear)." This applies to in-person bullying as well as trolling.

- Give direct feedback. They're likely to be defensive, but that doesn't mean you should be silent; just be prepared. You might want to use amenable language so they can save face, potentially reducing pushback. Words like "I'm sure you didn't intend to . . . ," "I'm guessing there's a good reason that . . . ," "I may be wrong, but . . ." Even if they don't own it, they're on alert they've been caught. Don't expect an apology or think an apology (if offered) is the same as mending their ways. Watch to see if their behavior changes, at least around you.

- Stay out of the gang. Use some of the advice from the Narcissistic Leader section about staying on the outskirts of the inner sanctum—be friendly but not an intimate.

- Redirect conversation. When the talk turns to gossip, say you'd rather talk about something else and change the subject. Chat about books, cat videos, pets, kids, travel, movies, food, music, the news—anything but other staff members. If you're included in a chat thread that gets into gossip, ask to have the thread restarted without your name on it. No one is safe if anyone is gossiped about.

- Consult but don't fix. Even if the Gang Leader has a change of heart, they typically don't know how to repair the damaged relationships they've created. If you have a good relationship with this person and are skilled at interpersonal relationships, you may be in a position to give advice about what they can do to make things better—particularly since you're intimately aware of the specifics of the situation. However, *do not* try to fix relationships for them, even if they implore you to do so. Remember, Gang Leaders are master manipulators and you don't want to get sucked into doing their bidding.

- Report repeated bullying or trolling to your manager or human resources.

How to Deal with a Gang Leader: Advice for Managers

- Make your expectations crystal clear for all your staff. It would be wise to have your expectations about interactions within the team (not just the technical work) in writing where everyone can see them. But most importantly you need to monitor adherence to these norms. The Gang Leader requires much closer scrutiny to assure their observance of these practices. Catch any backslides quickly and insist on course corrections. Unchecked behavior becomes the new normal.

- Be very careful about promotional opportunities for a Gang Leader. Some can thrive in a leadership position but only if they have enough emotional maturity to change their way of working with others and exhibit fairness to all. Let them know that they're required to demonstrate and sustain these skills *before* a promotion would be considered. Be particularly wary of advancing those who demonstrate bullying behaviors.

- Notice if there's a crack in their armor (for example, if they feel a need to justify their actions) because it might be a teachable moment. The more a person needs to justify their behavior, the more they're fighting with themselves about what's right versus what they did.

There may actually be a bud of empathy struggling to open. If you've got a good relationship with this person, it's of great service to help them connect with their moral compass.

- Be aware if informal leadership moves into bullying. As the manager, you have an obligation to intervene. Consult with human resources for advice if you have seen behavior (or it's been reported to you) that borders on bullying or coercion.
- Be alert to gang dynamics that can occur as a result of the work group being physically separated. There are special challenges when you manage a group of people who aren't co-located. It's not unusual for those in a satellite location to feel disconnected from the "mother ship." A similar dynamic may occur when part of the team works in a centralized location and the rest are remote workers. Watch out for "us versus them" sentiments whipped up by Gang Leaders. Call it out if you see it and reinforce the solidarity (mission, norms) of the entire team, regardless of where they may sit.

How to Deal with a Gang Leader: Advice for Skip-Level Managers (Their Boss's Boss)

Tread carefully when the Gang Leader comes to you—and they likely will. All employees should have access to their skip-level manager if they can't achieve resolution on issues with their own manager. No doubt you're aware if there's a Gang Leader in your line. Listen to their complaints carefully, but don't promise anything other than to speak with their boss to learn more. You want to see action on legitimate issues but not undercut the manager. Together, you and the direct supervisor need to create a plan. Don't allow the Gang Leader continued audience in your office to whine about their manager—send them back to that person or suggest that the three of you meet.

<><><><><><><><><><><><><><><><><><><><><><><><><><><><><><><><><><><><><><><><><><><>

WORKSHEET:

IF YOU THINK YOU MAY BE A GANG LEADER

Please answer the following questions with a yes or no. For each yes answer, see the advice that follows the question.

1. Have you been passed over for promotion, even though you believe you have the necessary skills and the support of a number of your coworkers?
Speak to your manager or an HR representative about what the qualifications are for promotional positions. Make sure to ask about the interpersonal skills needed, not just the technical skills, and ask for an honest assessment of how you stack up.

2. Are you highly critical of management and feel like you know better what they ought to do?
Being a Gang Leader is one way of exerting power, but being a naysayer is its dark side. You can demonstrate healthy power by using your influence to make things better in the team and the department. You might find it rewarding to effect improvements. Volunteer to assist with quality efforts or ask how you can help the manager with their priorities.

3. Have you been told (or are you aware) that you're an informal leader but pretend you don't have influence over others?
Influence is a gift to appreciate and use well. Think about doing more to help others than to help yourself. Can you mentor, coach, or in some other way positively affect your environment?

4. Have you been told you're a bully, or do you recognize these characteristics in yourself because you're aware that you want to hurt certain people?

There are aspects of being a Gang Leader that can border on (or be) bullying. Manipulating, criticizing, or shunning people are all examples of bullying. So is trolling. You might consider an apology to those you've hurt. An apology starts with, "I'm sorry for (whatever you said or did)," and then stops. This isn't an opening to continue on with a justification of your actions. The statement "in my defense" isn't part of an apology. If you're asked about what prompted what you did, you can state the conditions in a non-blaming manner (e.g., "because I felt stressed," *not* "because you made me feel stressed," which is blaming). If this is something that you want to change about how you interact with others, I highly recommend that you seek counseling for help and support.

5. Do you find yourself justifying your actions to convince yourself and others of your right to do what you did?

If you attempt to convince yourself it was okay to be mean or hurtful, or you create a story in which you were the victim to make yourself feel better, your moral compass is trying to assert itself even if you weren't asking for its direction. It's a sign of strength to reflect upon one's painful, not-so-proud moments and learn from them. What do you want to do differently in the future?

◇◇

The Dramatics and Non-Stop Talkers

As narcissists go, the Dramatic and Non-Stop Talker aren't particularly dangerous unless they have some of the attributes listed above. I've placed them in the Narcissistic Jerk chapter because typically they aren't tuned in to others but rather focused on themselves. Dramatics and Non-Stop Talkers have different behaviors but how you deal with them is similar, so I've lumped them together.

You'll recognize the Dramatic or Non-Stop Talker by the following characteristics:

- Many don't do well working in silence by themselves for any period of time.
- They may think that the way to bond with others is to talk about themselves, or worse, gossip.
- Dramatics need an audience to display their emotions. They are, well, dramatic. Tears and angry outbursts can switch to lavish praise and gratitude; all of it has a place in their repertoire. If they have meltdowns in private, I'm sure they post about it. Suffering in silence isn't their gift.
- Dramatics can be overly sensitive and fall apart over any perceived criticism.
- Non-Stop Talkers come in many stripes. One variety can be triggered by anxiety or silence. In either instance, the talker launches a verbal diversion and nervously babbles on.
- Other Non-Stop Talkers (as well as Dramatics) may be oblivious to conventional norms of sharing or cues they've spoken long enough. This becomes even more pronounced on virtual platforms when they take over and it becomes more difficult to cut them off.
- Some Non-Stop Talkers have trouble getting to the point; that's why they ramble. Or they just don't want to yield the floor to anyone else.
- Either type may also be dreamers painting a fanciful future or hooked on some get-rich-quick scheme. Their optimism can be contagious, even if their plan is outrageous.

What these two types have in common is their immunity to signals from you that you are busy, bored, anxious, or just need to get on with your life. The worst of them spread a black cloud of gossip, anger, disappointment, victimization, and worry. The best of them can be great entertainers. At either extreme (and everywhere in between), these people can suck up a lot of your work time.

Shondra's Suffering

Shondra came to talk to me about Palmer. Every time she walked by his cube, Palmer would call out. Shondra's a nice person; she didn't want to hurt Palmer's feelings, so she'd stop to say hi. Now that he had an audience, Palmer would begin his soliloquy. It would've been one thing if this was a three-minute monologue, but once he got going, he could ramble on for upwards of twenty minutes.

Shondra had started going to the restroom on another floor just to avoid walking by his cube. When she heard him coming (talking the entire way), she'd pick up the phone and motion to Palmer that she was going to be on the call awhile. Shondra knew this was a small thing, but Palmer's relentless tales were starting to make her dread going to work. I taught Shondra the art of the drive-by wave and "hi" with a friendly smile. The idea is to *keep moving*, even if you say a few words as you walk past, such as, "Hey, Palmer, good to see you."

How to Deal with Dramatics and Non-Stop Talkers

Not all of these people are jerks; you may actually enjoy them! But their inability to read cues, their loudness and endless verbalizations can get tiresome, not to mention take hours away from your work. If what you've already tried hasn't helped, some of these suggestions might:

- Limit your exposure. If you have to walk by them and they want to nab you, smile and say, "Hi, I've got to run." Or smile and wave, but *keep your momentum going forward*.
- Interrupt. The secret to interrupting is not to wait for a pause because there may never be one. Jump in and use their name. Since most of us pay attention to our name, you might say something like, "Palmer, I've got to go now. See you!" If you're on a virtual platform with them, you might try raising your hand either literally or by using an icon.
- Leave on your schedule. If you decide to stop and visit for a minute, be aware of how long you're there. When it's time to leave, go. When the virtual meeting is over, end the meeting before it devolves into a monologue.
- Stop being so nice. It's okay to state your needs and end the one-sided conversation: "I need to get back to work," "I really don't have time to talk right now," "I'm on a deadline."
- Don't waste your energy on being hurt because they aren't reciprocating; they may be impervious to taking turns. If you're waiting for them to ask how *you* are and listen to the answer, you may be waiting a very long time. It's fairly common for them to ask you a question that takes them right back to one more story about themselves.
- Borrow from the suggestions for dealing with the Gang Leader: switch the subject, then end the interaction.
- Take charge of your workspace. If they're in your space and you need them to leave, try saying, "Sorry, I need to get back to work," then move your eyes to what you were doing before you were interrupted. If that doesn't work, stand up, say you need to go to the restroom/see Dave/get to a meeting/find food,

then walk them out of your area and continue on your way.

- Be assertive with boundaries. If your Dramatic/Non-Stop Talker regularly interrupts the flow of meetings, ask the meeting leader if they've noticed a tendency for the meeting to get off track when Palmer starts talking. If the leader is reluctant to do anything about Palmer, and you're assertive enough to intervene, ask if it's okay if you interrupt a tangent. A statement like, "Palmer, I think we've strayed off the agenda," will provide an opening for the leader to get the meeting back on track. In the virtual space, you can raise your hand to interrupt and then deliver the message. Believe me, if you can get the meeting back on track, waves of gratitude will flow your way from other frustrated meeting participants.
- Provide feedback to the person about what they're doing and its impact on others. This is particularly helpful if you have a trusted relationship with them.
- Set a time to meet later to socialize. If you enjoy this person's conversation, get together for coffee or lunch, or set up a Zoom chat. If you're in-person, rendez-vous away from the work setting where you're paid to be productive.

◇◇

WORKSHEET:
IF YOU THINK YOU MAY BE A DRAMATIC
OR NON-STOP TALKER

Please answer the following questions with a yes or no. For each yes answer, see the advice that follows the question.

1. Do you ignore or fail to notice cues that others are bored or need to move on?

Body language is a good clue, so look for these: people's eyes drop or look away when you talk, they open their mouths to say something (but you chatter on), they continue to work, they start backing away from you physically, they're looking at their devices and texting. These are all opportunities for you to check in with your audience about whether they've something to say or you need to wrap it up.

Being aware of others' cues is more difficult in the virtual world, so you really need to pay attention to other people's faces and not be looking at yourself on screen. Notice if there are hands raised or others trying to speak and you talk over each other. Give them a turn.

2. Do you take up a lot of airtime and monopolize conversations?

Consider setting the goals of asking more questions and listening thoughtfully. Don't interrupt when someone else's story reminds you of a story about yourself. Instead, listen patiently, or ask questions to learn more. If you're afraid of forgetting your thought, you can jot down a few words to remind you.

3. Are you worried you waste a lot of time every day by socializing?

That's an indicator you probably are. Please note that you're not only wasting your time but others' as well. Don't you have work stacked up at your desk/inbox? You probably never thought of it this way, but taking time away from the work you're paid to do is actually stealing from your employer.

4. Is your topic of conversation "Woe is me," complaining about your situation at work or at home, or both?

Compassion from others is harder to come by if you're frequently telling a tale worthy of a country-western song (e.g., the truck broke down, you lost your job, your spouse left, and the dog died). If you find you're endlessly sounding like a victim, see the Poor Me Jerk chapter, the "Why Me?" section, for more information on what you might try.

5. Do you frequently feel the need to "vent" to colleagues to get things off your chest?

You may think it's okay when in reality it's a burden to your coworkers. Please be aware of what you're saying and to whom. Complaining via email is just as dreary. Venting easily turns into gossip when the other party adds to it and then passes it along. When it's in writing, you don't know where it will end up.

6. Do you interrupt a lot and leave a conversation with no new knowledge about the other person or their views?

That's a tip-off you're monopolizing the conversation. Stop yourself occasionally to ask a question of the other person, then pay attention. If you tend to interrupt with your own stories, you can reveal that you're working on this and ask that they put up a hand if they're not finished speaking. If you're given the sign to wait, banish your own story from your mind so you can hear them. A conversation isn't dueling monologues; it's an exchange of related ideas.

7. Do you tend to go on tangents in meetings or take the group off the agenda?

Enlist others' support. If you know you tend to get off track during meetings, ask a trusted ally to give you a signal that alerts you to stop. If your meetings are virtual, ask your ally to send you a private message if you've gone on long enough. Believe me, people will thank you for staying on topic so the meeting can wrap up.

8. Are you so uncomfortable with silence, or anything resembling conflict, that it drives you to intervene or speak?

Silence is okay. In fact, a lot of people need quiet to be able to think. You don't need to fill the space with talk. Work on lengthening the amount of time before you speak. Notice when you feel anxious, then add another one to two seconds of silence before jumping in.

If you feel you need to interrupt immediately because there's conflict, listen to what you're saying to yourself when you hear raised voices or differing points of view. If your internal dialogue is, "Danger!" you might be able to change it to, "I'm safe. They're exploring differences." If you have trouble with this, please consider counseling. There's more on this in the Fight-or-Flee Jerk chapter, the "Let's Make a Deal" section.

9. Do you feel the need to entertain people?

Entertainment is great if it isn't interrupting people and doesn't take a lot of time away from work—*and* your audience is interested. If you're interrupting people with your humor, you might check out the chapter "The Not-So-Funny Jokester," and limit the time you take away from your colleagues' work.

Summary for Dealing with Any Narcissistic Jerk

As described, narcissism exists on a spectrum. The commonality of this Jerketype is their self-absorption and lack of awareness, or lack of concern about their impact on others. The inability to be empathetic and the desire for control is largely characteristic of the Narcissistic Leader and the Gang Leader. Lower level narcissists like the Dramatics and the Non-Stop Talkers may like to hear themselves speak, entertain, or want to gain sympathy. They aren't nearly as dangerous as those who are out to gather groupies and turf. Please take care of yourself around the more dangerous narcissists.

Summary for Handling the Narcissistic Leader and Gang Leader:
- Recognize the situation for what it is and set your boundaries.
- Protect yourself politically and emotionally if they have the power to do you harm.
- Remain somewhat distant from the in-crowd, even if you don't like the feeling of being "unpopular."
- Get out of the situation if you are dragged down to the point that you are feeling helpless, hopeless, or sick.

Summary for Handling the Dramatic and/or Non-Stop Talker
- If you don't have time to talk, say so, or let your feet say it all by walking, or by ending the call or virtual meeting.
- If they stray, guide them back to the point of the meeting.
- If you like them, enjoy them when you aren't on the clock.
- If you've got a good relationship, consider giving them feedback about how they're coming across.

Chapter Three:

THE KNOW-IT-ALL JERK

B eing a Know-It-All isn't about having more intelligence than everyone else in the room. It isn't about being a vocal fan of some product or service. The people who win a place in the Know-It-All Jerk Hall of Fame manage to dance on our nerves by their pattern of: interrupting our good work to tell us how to do it better, meddling to be "helpful," providing endless unasked-for advice, going silent and glaring in negative judgment, needing an audience to reinforce their superiority, or engaging in battle for their "rightness"— sometimes in devious ways.

Over the years, I've worked with a number of brilliant people who *aren't* Know-It-All's. I'm in awe of their ability to be groundbreakers in their fields, lead discoveries, and provide the rest of us with an understanding that informs our decision-making. We rely on, and appreciate, experts. The Know-It-All may have expertise, but their boorish behavior diminishes the positive impact they could have.

There are a variety of Know-It-All Jerks. As with other Jerketypes, the distinctions among them can be blurry or mixed in with other characteristics—and there's always a spectrum.

In this chapter, we will cover:

- **The Know-It-All with Guru Tendencies** (Come sit at my feet and learn from the best.)
- **The Lone Wolf Team Member** (I'll do it my way.)
- **The Insufferable** (And another thing you should do . . .)
- **The Meddlesome Manager** (Why isn't that "t" crossed?)
- **The Gotcha** (I'm so disappointed in you . . .)

The Know-It-All with Guru Tendencies

There are legitimate roles for teachers and mentors. The initial agreement is the teacher provides information and recommendations to help the student become proficient, and the student wants what's offered. Good teachers know when to back away from giving advice so the mentored can fly on their own. In contrast, the Know-It-All with Guru Tendencies has expertise to share, but rather than share it freely (or even sell it), they make you beholden to them by extracting a psychological price.

Characteristics you might recognize:

- They adopt you as a their "cause."
- They want something in return. Payment for their wisdom can range from expecting repeated favors to needing you to provide them with excessive attention.
- They affirm their superiority. Some have a need to relentlessly remind you of your once-upon-a-time inferior knowledge and how they saved you.
- They seem to want adoration and to be an endless fountain of advice—desired or not.

Candace and Her Unrequested Guru

Candace showed up in my office frustrated by an older colleague, Doris, who continued to give her unsolicited advice. When she was new in her job, Candace needed to learn from Doris, who'd provided the requisite tutoring. A year later, Candace had graduated—she was completely proficient, and acknowledged as such by her boss. Doris, however, seemed blind to the fact that Candace no longer required her mentoring. Candace had tried to be nice about it, thanking her but saying she didn't need the assistance. Doris was offended that Candace wasn't more grateful and desirous to learn everything Doris had to offer. She kept reminding Candace of how far she'd come under her tutelage. Candace felt like she was being suffocated and had become Doris's adopted child. At team lunches, Doris spoke to her in a patronizing tone, often referring to Candace's youth. Candace wondered if she had a work issue, or a generational one, or both.

Since Candace was already saying, "No, thank you, I don't need the assistance," but hadn't addressed the disrespect at other times when she felt patronized, I suggested she find a moment alone with Doris the next time that happened. She could say something like, "I'm sure you're not aware of how much it bothers me when you mention my age as if it makes me incompetent. I'm not sure that's what you mean to say, but I'd appreciate it if you'd stop." She could also offer a suggestion that since Doris enjoyed teaching so much, she might talk with their manager about other opportunities to instruct or mentor.

I ran into Candace a while later and asked how things were. She said that Doris was surprised by the feedback and apologetic that her comments were heard as derogatory. She thought she was being funny. She agreed with Candace that she'd like to do more teaching and would follow up with their manager. Their peer relationship had moved to firmer ground.

How to Deal with the Know-it-All with
Guru Tendencies

- State your issue clearly and without blaming or shaming. It's possible that your person is unaware of how their actions affect you. Try giving clear and non-accusatory feedback like Candace did. Say something like, "I'm sure you're unaware that when you give me advice, I wonder if you think I'm inept," or "You probably don't mean to do this, but when you question how I spend my time, I feel like you're my parent." Then say what you do want, something like, "I'd really prefer to be on equal footing as coworkers," or "I'd like to be able to ask for your help but only when I need it."

- Call it out if necessary. Lack of awareness is one thing; putting you down by design is another. If you feel you're being underestimated so that someone else can feel superior, it's time to protect yourself. If you think it'd make a difference, you could say, "If I didn't know better, I'd think you were trying to belittle my work." At least they'd know you're onto them. Or, "I don't appreciate you diminishing my work." You may get a defensive reaction like, "That's not what I'm doing." No need to argue. A response of "huh" or "interesting" is enough. If they ask what they said or did, you have the opportunity to let them know specifically what they're doing that's offensive. This type of conversation is best accomplished in a private setting. If yours is a virtual relationship, have a phone call or virtual meeting rather than discussing this via email.

- Be gracious and accept an apology if offered. Even if there's no apology, allow the relationship to repair if their behavior changes. But if the pattern starts up again, you may have to go through the steps you used before.

- Be appropriately grateful. Giving thanks to the person who has helped you is polite; feeding their ego with excessive flattery is not required.
- Avoid being baited. If you think you're being treated as if you're ignorant as a way to get under your skin and provoke an angry response, arguing about how capable you are is unlikely to make any difference. It's a game, so stop playing. Don't respond (if your body language shows anger, that's still responding), or change the subject. See if you can let provocative comments roll off your back with a thought like, "That's just Doris."
- Discuss the issue with your manager. If this is a colleague with whom you have attempted to draw the line but have been unsuccessful, you may want to let your manager know you're having difficulty with continued advice giving and how it's affecting your work. Let them know what you've already tried and ask for suggestions.
- If this *is* your manager, see the Meddlesome Manager section for tips.
- Seek additional help for generational issues. If you believe the root of the problem rests in generational differences, there are some great books, videos, and articles on this topic. Do a search to find them. They're updated regularly with the changing age composition of the workforce (see the Additional Resources section).

〈◇◇◇〉

WORKSHEET:

IF YOU THINK YOU MAY BE A KNOW-IT-ALL

WITH GURU TENDENCIES

Please answer the following questions with a yes or no. For each yes answer, see the advice that follows the question.

1. Is it possible your audience isn't interested in the information you wish to share?
It's terrific that you have a body of knowledge that you want to share—just be sure they want it. If your chosen person to instruct is telling you to back off verbally or through their body language, do!

2. If your manager has asked you to teach a colleague, are you aware of the scope?
Clarify with your manager if you're to teach the basics of how to do specific tasks or provide more complex instruction (like everything you've ever learned about the job). Make sure you're clear on the assignment and that your pupil is too. Ask the manager if they can address the expectations to both of you at the same time.

3. Is the student having trouble mastering the skills you're teaching?
It may be your instructional style. See the "Unknowing, Unskilled, and Left-to-Languish" section of the Incompetent Jerk chapter.

4. Are you trying to force-feed an entire career's worth of experience into someone else?
While you may feel you're not being asked to go as deeply

into the skills that you believe are necessary for success in the long term, remember that you didn't learn what you know in a month, or even five years. They'll be gaining their own wisdom over the course of their career. Focus on the skills they need now and ask what they would most like to learn from you.

5. Do you know when it's time to let your mentee fly on their own?

Anticipate how you'll know that time has come, and when it does, let it be a celebration for both of you. If you're mentoring someone, and not just teaching a skill or orienting to a job, establish a time frame at the beginning of the relationship so you'll both know when it's time to reevaluate or conclude (e.g., a year's commitment).

6. Do you say things to your younger coworkers as if you're an older (and annoying) relative?

Statements like, "I have socks older than you," or "You'll understand when you're as old as I am," or "I've been doing this since you were in grade school," are offensive and dismissive.

7. Do you fail to notice and solicit the experience of your younger colleagues?

Look for their gifts; you might learn something yourself. They'll be more receptive to your lifetime of experience if you treat them respectfully and let them initiate coming to you for advice. Let the mentee decide if they want to continue the relationship over time. Be willing to morph from "guru" to peer.

8. Do you treat older colleagues as though they have nothing to offer and are hopelessly out-of-date?

You may have more skill and facility in some areas, but they have more skill and experience in others. Look for what they have to offer and focus on that. Be patient when they need more time or assistance with new skills, particularly technology.

9. Do you get a large part of your self-esteem from having acolytes?

Beware of this type of ego-gratification. It's easy for a popular teacher to believe all the positive comments that come from adoring students and effortlessly slide into guru status. The best teachers continue to learn and are transparent about their areas of growth. Remind yourself to stay humble even in the face of praise from students.

◇◇

The Lone Wolf Team Member

It's not surprising that a single Know-It-All team member who refuses to play well with others can have a dramatic impact on the work and morale of a team. The Lone Wolf is highly driven toward goal achievement. Their impatience with group process can leave a trail of damaged relationships. What the Lone Wolf fails to recognize is that those same team members, if ticked off, can retaliate and/or refuse to work with them in the future.

How you can recognize a Lone Wolf:

- They believe they're the single authority and the end justifies the means—no matter what.
- They can nod their head in agreement and (as if they had their fingers crossed behind their back) go off and do it their way.
- They're not always who they appear to be, and not all Lone Wolves are equal. Yours may, or may not, be an expert. Sometimes they talk a good game but don't really have the goods.

- They won't readily share information. They'll cherry-pick what they want you to know and leave out the rest. If you're their supervisor, you know how difficult they can be to manage.
- They want to move fast, and a team just slows them down.

Miscast Mark

The leader of a project team, Kris, came to me about Mark. Mark was an expert on the specifics of one particular system that was being evaluated, among others. Mark's budget would be tapped for the system installation; however, there were ongoing costs and maintenance that other departments would need to bear.

Mark's two biggest failings were his disregard of others' knowledge and opinions and his subversion of group process in his desire to go it alone. He wasn't concerned that his decisions and actions impacted others' work and budgets downstream—he had opinions about what they should do too. According to Mark, if they followed his advice all would be well. He used a morally superior tone, arguing why his preferred system was the only correct choice. Some of these characteristics echo those of the Narcissistic Jerk, whose mantra is, "It's all about *me*." Mark's Lone Wolf mantra was, "It's all about what I *know*."

I counselled Kris to be clear about the decision-making process and get agreement from each team member. When Kris reported back, she said that Mark, along with everyone else, said yes to the process. After a number of meetings, they were making steady progress toward a purchase decision. Then Mark got impatient. He did an end run and worked alone with his preferred vendor since the group seemed to be leaning in that direction. By acting solo, he committed the team (and organization) to a contract for services and timeline. Understandably, his team members were furious about not being included.

Mark broke the trust of the team by disregarding the agreed-upon rules. It wasn't that his vendor choice was unworkable, but his failure to include others meant that they didn't get everything they needed. This major gaffe, on top of multiple shouting matches with colleagues, led to Mark's mutually-agreed-upon departure from the company.

How to Deal with the Lone Wolf

- Appeal to the Lone Wolf through logic and use "thinking" words. Emotional appeal and "feeling" words don't work very well. It's the difference between "I think" and "I feel."
- Be prepared. If your Lone Wolf has shown their colors before and you know the risk of their running alone is high, talk about it before it happens. Use language like, "I'm sure you have the best interests of the company in mind; however, the consequences of working independently could be damaging and costly. I expect you to work with the team."
- Establish guidelines. Make sure they're aware of when they must involve others in decisions or actions, particularly if they are working remotely. It's too easy for the Lone Wolf to move forward on their own if they aren't co-located with most of the team. Be particularly alert to messages like, "I went ahead with this because I didn't want to bother the team."
- Call them on their actions, especially if they fly in the face of agreements the team made. This is best done in person (no flaming emails, please), and without an audience. Because they're far less interested in maintaining relationships than they are in achieving results, emphasize the negative impact to the *work*, not just to you (or the team) personally.
- Assign work based on their strengths. If you're this

person's manager, realize that their tendency to act on their own may be moderated but is unlikely to change. Play to their strengths by assigning them work where they do have ultimate authority. Then set up clear guidelines and have frequent check-ins. Or retain them as external consultants where you have control over the parameters of the project and how their expertise is used.

- Manage your own emotions. If repeated transgressions by your Lone Wolf send you down the path of anger, make sure you look for their positive qualities too: knowledge, dedication, support of the mission, great research, whatever it is they offer. Give the required negative feedback, but don't lose sight of their contributions.

⋙⋘⋙⋘⋙⋘⋙⋘⋙⋘⋙⋘⋙⋘⋙⋘⋙⋘⋙⋘⋙⋘⋙⋘⋙⋘⋙⋘

WORKSHEET:

IF YOU THINK YOU MAY BE A LONE WOLF

Please answer the following questions with a yes or no. For each yes answer, see the advice that follows the question.

1. Do you underestimate your team members' contributions?
You may think you're the expert, but if they have differing opinions from yours, listen to learn versus listening to defend your point of view. They may have something valuable to offer that you're missing.

2. Do you use detrimental team tactics, such as acting on your own without informing anyone?
You might get a pass once, but after that, folks won't be so forgiving. Identify what happens that sends you on a solo

flight. Is it when decision-making is shared that you become impatient? Do you decide for other team members that you'll save them the trouble and do it yourself? Make a plan to do something different to assure you work within your team instead of working parallel to it. If, for example, you recognize that shared decision-making is a trigger for you, talk yourself down and participate—even if you think that you'd make a better and faster decision on your own.

3. Are you in a job where teamwork is a requirement?

Most jobs rely on teams and for that you need collaboration skills. What consistent feedback have you been given about your work style? That's a place to start. You may need to learn how to productively engage with others. I applaud your courage to examine team-busting tendencies. Moving from a need-to-control to a shared-control approach isn't easy; you may want to seek assistance from a therapist or coach.

The Insufferable

Those who can't stop themselves from giving advice on all manner of topics have a good dose of Non-Stop Talker Narcissist blended with being a Know-It-All. They've found every product or remedy that you must have. They have an opinion about everything, and they believe they're the ultimate resource.

Other ways you might recognize them:

- They know what *you* should do and must share that knowledge.
- They have zero curiosity about your experience because they believe they're smarter and wiser than everyone else.

- They make grand declarations about quality, price, and convenience, without regard to your circumstances or resources.
- They may be completely misguided or misinformed yet are deaf to facts that contradict their beliefs. They'll cut you off and continue their monologue.
- They are missing some critical skills (like reading their audience). At work they have ample opportunities to spew their overflowing stream of advice at breaks, between meetings, before meetings, on email, and in the hallway. This is probably the person you avoid in social settings.

Generous-with-Advice Jennifer

I was at a multiday conference where we were assigned seating for the keynote lunch. Our table of eight was comprised of strangers, so we introduced ourselves, where we were from, and our company affiliations. I was seated next to Jennifer.

As luck would have it, I was the only one from the Pacific Northwest at the table. Jennifer had visited Seattle once, which provided a starting point for conversation. Within two minutes it became clear that Jennifer's self-appointed job was to inform me where to go in my own city for an excellent meal, the best pedicure, fine theater, discount shopping, and the most breathtaking views of the Sound.

Not finished after completing her tour of my home-town's businesses and amenities, she went on to tell me how to buy, and through whom I should purchase, travel insurance for myself and supplemental health insurance for my mother—and who had the best cell phone plans. Early on in her monologue, I foolishly suggested a Seattle restaurant that I think is wonderful. I was dismissed with a wave, and on she went. I glazed over. I know I stared dumbly at her before focusing on my plate, hoping that the floor would open and swallow the verbose Jennifer—or me. Needing no eye contact to keep up her stream of advice, she marched on until, blessedly, the keynote speaker was introduced.

How to Deal with the Insufferable

- Speak up. Is this someone you spend a lot of time with and otherwise like? If so, it might be worth being assertive and letting them know how crazymaking it is to have them tell you what you should do. If it's a lack of awareness that drives their endless fountain of advice, that might dry it up. If they want to keep the relationship, they're likely to try to make some adjustments.
- Politely reject their advice. Another assertive response is, "Thanks, but I think we have different tastes/opinions/perspectives." If it comes via email, feel free to delete it.
- Grin and bear it. If this is an encounter of short duration, this might be the easiest choice.
- Focus your attention elsewhere. Fortunately, at work there are natural endings to conversation: the start of the meeting, someplace you need to be, or work you must complete. Or you can look for a convenient excuse ("Oh, there's Doug!") and walk off quickly as if you've been waiting to speak to him all day. If you're on a virtual meeting, you can look at your phone (as if it started to ring on silent mode) and say, "Excuse me, I need to take this," and leave the meeting.
- Distance yourself. If it's an informal gathering where you can mix and mingle (such as a birthday or retirement party), move on. The social rule is that it's okay to drop away from a conversation to speak with someone else. If you're one of several people held hostage, you can move off. If you're the only one collared, you can excuse yourself with something like, "Interesting thoughts, Jennifer. I'm going to get another drink/get

some food/say hello to some people." Then walk away.

- Interrupt and divert attention. If you are stuck at a table together, try suggestions from the previous chapter for dealing with the Non-Stop Talker, and interrupt. Then turn your attention elsewhere (such as the person seated on your other side). You can also keep your ears open for something that others at the table are talking about and interrupt with something like, "I'd really like to hear what Geoff is saying about gorillas," and join that conversation.

- Finally, there's the tried-and-true, get-up-and-go-to-the-restroom solution. From there you are free to roam the room. That's what I should have done with Jennifer.

⟨⟨⟨

WORKSHEET:

IF YOU THINK YOU MAY BE AN INSUFFERABLE

Please answer the following questions with a yes or no. For each yes answer, see the advice that follows the question.

1. Do you engage in monologues?

What's driving that? If it's insecurity or not being comfortable with a moment of silence, start working on your conversational skills by asking questions about others' experiences. Increase your tolerance for silence. Some people need a moment to think before they speak. Don't jump in to add your two cents; wait and listen.

2. Do you miss signs that you've spoken too long?

People give subtle, and not-so-subtle, cues when they want to speak or interject a thought. The subtle cues are when someone takes a breath, leans forward, and closes their mouth as if ready to form a word. The obvious cue is actually speaking: "No, but," "In my experience," "Have you thought of . . ." If you notice that you've cut someone off, stop and say, "I'm sorry. You had something to add." Then be quiet and don't interrupt. If you're speaking more than half the time, you might want to pay attention to listening more. If you're on a virtual meeting and find people are speaking over you, that's a signal to stop talking.

3. Have you become a social pariah to the point that people avoid you?

Talking incessantly about your superior knowledge moves you firmly in that direction. It is read as arrogant. Things to do: ask more questions, hold back your own thoughts, use fewer words, stop occasionally, and read your audience for signs they've had enough. An obvious indicator is if someone jumps in and changes the subject during a brief moment of silence.

4. Do you feel compelled to give advice?

Needing to be in charge of what everyone else "ought" to do is a heavy burden. Put it down. Let people figure things out on their own—unless they ask you for your thoughts. Compulsive advice giving can damage relationships and cause you to lose friends. Don't expect people to thank you or read obsessively forwarded email that *you* think they should read.

5. Do you have expertise that you want to share?

Turn your discoveries into a book, blog, articles, posts, podcasts, or reviews so people with similar interests can seek you out. Or be an expert speaker to groups that are interested in your topic.

The Meddlesome Manager

People moving into management positions seldom receive adequate preparation. Regardless of the nature of the business, most are promoted because they excelled in their previous work. The problem is that they're leaving a job they knew and did well for a job they don't know how to do. They're expected to perform, with little or no help in developing managerial skills. If they don't understand what the daily work of their new role entails, they slip right back into their comfort zone: doing the actual work of the staff they supervise. Sometimes even seasoned managers retain this maddening habit of taking over their employees' work.

You may identify this type by some of the following traits:

- They have excessive rules.
- They aren't clear about their expectations, so it's impossible to meet them.
- They have one way to do things: their way.
- They nitpick.
- They frequently criticize and infrequently praise.
- They may be constantly watching (or conversely, rarely watching), then suddenly pounce and critique.

A manager who takes away your ability to think, act, or be creative by telling you exactly what to do and how to do it can leave you disheartened. So can being criticized on a regular basis. This is what we call "seagull management"—swooping in, crapping on everything, then flying away. It leaves one to wonder, "Why bother if everything I do is wrong?"

Jorge and His Fussy Boss, Tina

Jorge contacted me to talk about a problem. He'd been in his job a couple of years when the manager left and the department of four was dispatched to remote work. A colleague,

Tina, was promoted into the manager position, and Jorge was happy for her. They'd gotten along fine when they were peers, and Jorge had relied on her for her depth of experience.

However, in the past six months everything had changed. He wasn't sure if it was moving to remote work that was so difficult for Tina, her new role, or both. Jorge found himself frequently in trouble by not meeting Tina's unstated standards. She insisted on seeing most of his customer communication before it was sent out, something his previous manager hadn't required. Tina often found picky things to criticize.

With each correction, it appeared that Tina's confidence in Jorge's ability eroded. His opportunities to take on more challenging assignments waned. The warm camaraderie they'd had as a team was gone. The only communication he had with his other two colleagues was via email and in a once-a-week virtual meeting. Tina drove the agenda, so they didn't have much opportunity to interact. Jorge found himself increasingly angry and frustrated. He'd snapped at Tina on more than one occasion and was now looking at job postings.

Jorge and I talked about the major changes that had collided at the same time: moving out of the office and a new manager. It was likely Tina was still finding her way with both her role and supervising from afar. There were, however, some things Jorge could do to help himself. Was there any pattern to what Tina identified as a problem? If he wasn't sure, he could ask and correct those issues. He could ask if the virtual meeting agendas could include time for conversation among the staff members to problem solve and catch up with each other. When Tina wanted to review his routine work, he could mention that he'd noticed that she often had critical comments—did she have different expectations from their previous manager? Each of these questions was designed to not only obtain information but also give subtle feedback to (the potentially unaware) Tina about what she was doing—and her impact on Jorge.

How to Deal with the Meddlesome Manager

Something about being told what to do, or being closely monitored, brings out the inner adolescent in most of us—we want to be truculent in return. If you act out, however, the opportunity to turn things around becomes severely compromised. Stay the adult person you are and try some of the following:

- Ask if their corrections are about substance or style. If it's style, ask if there's any reason you can't use your own versus theirs.
- Ask them to clarify what you have the authority to do on your own and what must be done in a prescribed way—or must have their approval.
- Ask your anxious manager who doesn't seem to trust you what you need to do to satisfy them that you're competent in your job.
- Ask questions about where your work products go if you don't already know. Your manager may be nervous because your material is sent on to the next level boss. For a new manager like Tina, that could be intimidating. If that's the case, ask how much review time your manager needs to conduct a quality check so they're comfortable sending it up the chain.
- Reflect on your past work experience and what brings out the best in you as an employee. Share this with your supervisor, not as a demand but as something you think might be of interest since they care about the team and the department. See if you can find compromises for the areas that have been bugging you.
- Consider other options within the company. If you are really bothered by the constant meddling but love the

work, you might look for another position in the company and wait for this manager to mature or leave. Come back to the department later, under better circumstances.

- Find another job. If you *really* can't stand it, it's better to get out than to burn bridges with angry standoffs about your boss's lack of skill or grace. You don't know what the future might bring; you might need this person's recommendation. Or, as fate sometimes has it, you could end up becoming this person's boss.

◇◇

WORKSHEET:

IF YOU THINK YOU MAY BE A

MEDDLESOME MANAGER

Please answer the following questions with a yes or no. For each yes answer, see the advice that follows the question.

1. Is this your first management position?

This is the time when you're in danger of being a micromanager because it's too easy to do the work that you used to do so well. Your management role is a different job and requires new skills. Speak with your manager (or peer managers) about what your new role entails and what training is available to you.

2. If someone on your team isn't doing their job well, do you do it for them?

It's tempting to do that, but that's micromanaging. What's much more beneficial is to teach and coach your staff person so they become proficient. If you need ideas, look in the Incompetent Jerk chapter, the "Unknowing, Unskilled, and Left-to-Languish" section.

3. Are you only calling out mistakes?

Look for what people are doing well and comment on it—using specifics. People need to hear "warmer," not just "colder." For example, "Jorge, I really liked the way you handled that complaint call. When the customer thanked you for your excellent service, I knew that you'd gained her loyalty to our company."

The Gotcha

There are people who have expectations of perfection that, unsurprisingly, aren't met. When it's you who has failed to deliver, you'll feel the heat. You can end up feeling surprised, hurt, and wonder what just happened. The words may be reasonable, but the tone is parental disappointment.

Other tip-offs that you've met this type:

- They may have a mild-mannered tone or demeanor—although some may attack. Either way, the results are the same: the problem is you or the circumstances, never them.
- They tend to be both control freaks and perfectionists. I'm sure they can't meet their own expectations.
- They can bring down any celebration or event by their evaluation that things aren't exactly right: "If only the music weren't so loud . . . ," "If they hadn't put so much cheese on it . . ."

The problem is there's just enough truth in what they say (or they hit a vulnerable spot) that you're left feeling uneasy or questioning your own competence. Their part in the drama is left unsaid, naturally.

Reasonable, Yet Vicious, Raquel

I responded to a call from Yasmin asking if I could join her and her boss, Dan, in her office—immediately. I dashed over to find the two of them reviewing the incident that had just occurred. It seems Yasmin's peer manager, Raquel, had been engaged in a whispering campaign with her staff against Yasmin. Raquel wanted to undermine Yasmin's reputation in the hope their boss would assign both departments to her.

Raquel could appear to be very rational and reasonable, so her staff tended to believe her. If Yasmin's and Raquel's departments hadn't worked so closely together, the subversion might have gone unnoticed by Yasmin. But they were co-located, consequently the staff of both intermingled, and then the rumors began to fly. When Dan got wind of the destructive dynamic, he confronted Raquel.

Dan was a seasoned director. He knew how to communicate what he wanted and monitor results. He was also incredibly busy, so even with the best intentions, there were missteps in following up. The case of Raquel was one of those.

A month ago, Dan had done Raquel's performance review, rating her as "needs improvement" in her peer relationships. Dan was aware of Raquel's tendency to dump on Yasmin and her staff's successes and to take credit where none was due. He'd assigned a project for Raquel and Yasmin to work on together. When Dan asked Yasmin about their progress, there'd been none because Raquel kept canceling meetings.

Right before they called me, they'd had their weekly management team meeting. Dan had confronted the issue of the stalled project. Raquel flew off the handle declaring that she was victimized by Dan's consistently poor management and had been undermined by gossip from Yasmin and her team (a projection of what *she'd* been doing). Her rant continued on about how work conditions had gone so far downhill under Dan's leadership. Raquel announced she needed to leave for the rest of the day due to emotional duress. She stormed out of the office, leaving Dan and Yasmin stunned.

Both of them were questioning themselves: what had they done wrong, what were they unaware of that they should have known, and were they terrible leaders? My only comment was, "Wow, she's good; look at what she's got you doing!" They both laughed. Then we evaluated what was feedback to pay attention to and what was a firestorm of deflection.

I suspected that Raquel's furious attack was a skill honed from an early age. Her explosion did exactly what it was intended to do: divert critical attention away from her and onto them. Dan decided to engage in a disciplinary process for Raquel, with strict outcomes to be met within a month. He assumed this would either result in Raquel's resignation or her termination from the company if she couldn't (or wouldn't) meet the expectations. It seemed Raquel had an ace in her back pocket because the next Monday she announced she was leaving for a new position.

How to Deal with a Gotcha

- If it happens rarely, let it go. The element of surprise is one of the most difficult aspects of the Gotcha. In your stunned state, you aren't equipped to respond. If it's a one-off situation, that's just how it is, so let it go and move on with your life. If it happens regularly, practice a response.
- If there's a pattern to their disapproval, have a ready reply. Example: "I've noticed that you bring up what you wished had happened during a meeting at the very end when there's no chance to do anything about it."
- Ask about their intention. If you're not sure what they're trying to say but you know you feel attacked, try saying something like, "Did you intend to criticize me?" If the answer is no, you can follow up with, "I'm

not sure what you were trying to say. Can you clarify?" If the answer is yes, they did mean to be critical, you can follow up with, "Would you be more specific about what it is that you think I failed to do?" Then you can decide if it's a fair critique or not.

- It may be that the tone is more problematic than the content. If the words seem reasonable but the manner is demeaning, say something like, "I'm not sure if you're aware of it, but the tone you used with me was very (patronizing/parental/judgmental/lecturing, etc.). It makes it hard for me to hear what you're saying/asking of me." This is best done in a one-on-one situation, not in front of a group.
- Beware the tendency to gossip about this person. If you've been victimized by a Gotcha Jerk, it's easy to want to spew to colleagues. Better to address your concern with the person involved than to spread negativity.

WORKSHEET:

IF YOU THINK YOU MAY BE A GOTCHA

Please answer the following questions with a yes or no. For each yes answer, see the advice that follows the question.

1. Did you learn to be judgmental early in your life, or maybe one of your parents was a Gotcha?

In that case, it's possible that you're unaware of how you come across because it seems normal. Your clues that this is a problem are in how people respond to you (i.e., hurt or upset) and how often your high expectations aren't met.

2. Have staff members who report to you, or peer colleagues, quit as a result of the tone you use?

If you're disappointed in people and use a demeaning tone with them, don't be surprised if they quit or find other assignments away from you. You might want to get assistance from a coach who can help you moderate your tone.

3. Are you disappointed in most situations, and feel the need to mention it?

Please understand what a downer that is, especially when others have worked hard to create an enjoyable experience. Even if you judge things as lacking, you can keep your mouth firmly closed.

4. Do you wait to state your concerns until it's too late?

Bring up issues when they can be resolved, not when it's minutes before the meeting adjourns or the plane takes off. If you do bring up a concern, be specific, and ask for the other person's perspective. Involve them in creating a solution.

5. Do you get something out of constantly being disappointed?

Some possibilities are: attention, a reputation of being discerning or being more knowledgeable or skilled than others because you always see what's wrong. You might want to review the Guru section of this chapter.

6. Are you the only person who does things right?

If that's so, it's time to question your judgment (and look at the Narcissistic Jerk chapter). Look for what other people do that's *good*, not just for what you think is substandard. Your way of doing things is one way. There are often multiple methods that get the same result.

Summary for Dealing with Any Know-It-All Jerk

A surefire solution to your angst is through managing *your* reaction to their irritating behavior. Here are some ideas:

- Engage in selective listening; take from their stream of advice that which might be useful and ignore the rest.
- Remove yourself from the situation if you're in danger of exploding.
- Ask yourself why you're allowing someone else to determine your mood. Change your thinking if you are increasingly upset with a colleague. Rather than getting infuriated by a boorish comment, use it as a cue to breathe deeply and remind yourself how lucky you are not to be related to/married to/living with this person.
- Take a more philosophical approach. Instead of engaging in an internal rant ("I'm sick to death of this!"), try switching your words ("That's just Raj doing his thing again."). Then let it roll off you. Maintaining a healthy blood pressure may depend on it.
- Choose where to put your attention. If you catch yourself ruminating about how awful this person is, stop and consciously choose to think of something else. Anger can be energizing, so we often resist letting it go. The downside is that these repeated thoughts create what I call a "neuro-rut" in the mind, continuing to feed your upset. Determine in advance what you'll think about instead—or what you'll use as a distraction. If you catch yourself thinking dark thoughts, initiate your plan. In my worst ruminating moments, I look for the color red in my environment. Anything can work as a distraction; the point is to break your thought pattern.

- Find something positive about this person and focus on that. Your Know-It-All may be an expert—what can you learn from them? My coping strategy with one jerk was to determine that each day I would look for something admirable about her knowledge. I had been so focused on the negative, I was convinced she couldn't even breathe right. For the duration of our work relationship, my change of focus changed my demeanor; I was less negative, thereby less miserable (and less miserable to be around!).

- Take the chance of giving direct feedback if the relationship is good otherwise. "Shondra, the amount of advice you give me is getting on my nerves. I really like you, but this is in the way." If Shondra agrees she'd like to work on it, she may be open to receiving a signal from you when she forgets. Breaking habits is hard; there will be slipups, so be patient.

- Check in with your boss. Have you been assigned a Know-It-All to teach you? If you feel you don't need this person's help, ask your boss what they see in your work that requires tutoring. If this assistance truly isn't needed, perhaps you can get your manager to agree to "call off the dogs."

- Stay aware of your team's needs. If you're the boss and dealing with a Lone Wolf, remain vigilant for any sabotage to the group's efforts if the Lone Wolf goes off on their own.

- Identify your options. If you are unable to morph what currently feels intolerable into the merely irritating (or, better yet, neutral), what are the potential consequences to you/your health/your relationships? What's your likely future in this department or organization if nothing (most importantly, you) changes? Act accordingly.

Chapter Four:

THE INCOMPETENT JERK

Depending on your personality, you may be more or less willing to give colleagues' poor work performance a pass. If you're an amiable type, you'll probably assist this person, and it doesn't get under your skin to do so—unless it goes on too long. If you're more like me, working side by side with someone who doesn't know what they're doing gets on your nerves.

Two issues that should push you to take action are:

- Concerns about physical or psychological safety that affect customers and/or colleagues.
- The damage that may be done by their continued lack of skill.

It's important to remember that your definition of what constitutes poor performance may not be in alignment with what your boss thinks. In the absence of clear and measurable standards, incompetence is in the eye of the beholder.

It's worthwhile to conduct a self-assessment about your own motives in labeling someone as incompetent. Maybe you want them to go away. Maybe you want to feel superior. Is it truly a job performance issue, or is it possible you don't like the person so it's easy to dismiss them as incompetent?

Assuming that your colleague truly isn't doing well in their job, there are a variety of reasons why this can happen:

- They're a poor match for the position.
- They didn't get good training from the start.
- The job became more complicated and they couldn't (or wouldn't) keep up.
- They've been given no (or confusing) performance expectations, and little or no feedback.
- They're emotionally immature and/or can't handle stress.
- They've been "Peter Principled" (promoted to a position above their competence).

Whether the coworker in question is aware that they're incompetent or not varies. Here are some possibilities:

- They're in over their heads, so they try to keep a low profile and hope the boss won't notice—and hang onto whatever self-esteem they can.
- They have such low expectations of themselves they don't aspire to do any better.
- They have no perspective. Even in the face of contrary evidence, they think they're doing well when they aren't.
- They're completely unaware they should be performing at a higher level.
- They may actually be doing the minimum required, but *you* have higher standards and (as a consequence) you find their performance lacking.
- They don't seem to care that they can't do the job and instead want to manipulate the system.

In this chapter we'll explore the following Incompetent Jerks and what you can (and, likely, *can't*) do about them:

- The Square Peg in a Round Hole (in the wrong job)
- The Unknowing, Unskilled, and Left-to-Languish (given no feedback or help)
- The Infuriatingly Incompetent Boss: screw-up managers in three parts—Unmanageable (doing it my way, regardless), Explosive (kaboom!) and Unqualified, or Uncaring (ineffectual for some unexplained reason)

The Square Peg in a Round Hole Incompetent

The lack of attention we give to selecting people for jobs is shameful. Would you ask someone to marry you based on an online profile? Well, I guess some would . . . however, we typically spend more time with coworkers than we do with our families. Those who do the hiring look at résumés and expect that tells the full story. Or figure that an advanced degree in a subject is qualification enough. They may have a thirty-minute Skype interview, and as long as the applicant isn't literally on fire, they get hired. Bad on us!

If you've ever been the manager responsible for hiring a poor match (and I have been, much to my chagrin), you know how painful it is for everyone. Most of my advice for dealing with the Square Peg in a Round Hole incompetent worker is directed to managers. However, if you're working side by side with someone who's in the wrong job, the following may give you some understanding, as well as ideas of what you can do.

Square Pegs may be recognized by the following:

- Exhibiting performance deficits that weren't apparent because essential skills were insufficiently screened during the interview process.

- Having an inflated sense of how they're doing, even when shown their errors.
- Deflecting your attention away from their incompetence by doing less important things (such as cleaning the breakroom) to avoid the required duties of the job.
- Resisting certain tasks while talking instead about how successful they were in a previous position—as if this makes up for their current lack of performance.
- Training that takes an inordinately long time, and their work is never completely satisfactory. Guidance continues to be needed on basic tasks.

Lucinda's Luck

Gerry, a seasoned manager, came to me about Lucinda. She'd hired into an entry-level position in the department, a position he'd hired for successfully many times over the years. Previous hires had been promoted to more responsible positions within two to four years.

Lucinda looked like she had the all the requisite administrative experience from former jobs: customer service, office organization, and bookkeeping. She'd demonstrated good social skills during the interview, so Gerry thought she'd fit in with the team and the customers. Wrong. Nine months into it, Lucinda still couldn't do the job without error and by now had ticked off a set of frequent customers. She couldn't remember the basic preferences of her most important clients. These people were complaining to Gerry saying they didn't want to work with Lucinda anymore.

I asked Gerry how long it took most people to become proficient in the job—six months. He was flummoxed. He reexamined her training. He arranged to have her review specific tasks with her colleagues who'd previously held the position. He had twice-a-week check-ins with her.

While Gerry intended the extra help to be of assistance, Lucinda saw it differently and complained she was being harassed. She became increasingly upset at being given instruction and blamed her boss for her mistakes. She said she didn't have enough training and attention from him, at the same time he was demonstrating exactly the opposite.

During the eighth month of her tenure, Lucinda had made a very costly error—not once but twice. It was unclear whether she couldn't, or wouldn't, do the work. She announced she was so stressed by the situation that she'd started counseling. Now she left early two days a week for therapy appointments.

Gerry had believed he was as a good manager who hired well and now his self-image was challenged, plus he'd never fired anyone. He wanted to make sure he'd done everything possible to help Lucinda be successful. He told me that she'd recently hinted she expected a promotion at her one-year employment anniversary.

No one is immune from making bad hiring decisions, even a seasoned manager. I asked Gerry when he knew that Lucinda wasn't catching on like his other new hires—at the end of the first six weeks. He kept thinking if he just hung in a little longer, Lucinda would "get it." Meanwhile, everyone else was having to pick up the work that wasn't getting done and make corrections to Lucinda's attempts. By the time I saw Gerry, he was doing a third of her work, which was fine by her. I assured him that he'd provided ample opportunities for training and coaching with multiple people; it seemed he had the wrong person in the job. Lucinda needed a performance improvement plan (PIP) that required a rapid and complete turnaround in her job performance—or she'd have to find a more suitable opportunity elsewhere.

As it turned out, when the PIP was presented, Lucinda made it clear she wasn't interested in changing anything to keep her job. She saved face by finding another job before she could be fired, but she continued to complain about Gerry (to anyone who would listen) all the way out the door.

How to Deal with a Square Peg in a Round Hole: Advice for Managers

- Avoid hiring them! If you're the manager who brought them in, you're part of the problem. Before interviewing candidates, clarify the most important skills and attributes required for the job. Learn how to conduct a behavioral based interview. This involves asking about specific situations from the candidate's past in which they've demonstrated the skills you seek (see the Additional Resources section). It's far more difficult to train a skill for which the person has little ability than it is to hire a person who shines in these areas. If you inherited this person when you became the manager, look for help in the "Unknowing, Unskilled, and Left-to-Languish" section of this chapter.

- Specify expectations for their work, set a time frame for when they should be able to adequately perform certain duties, and provide training. The training plan should include target dates for proficiency. If they can't perform to the measures you've set, you will both know it's time for a change.

- Provide appropriate training. Who's training this person? Do they have interest and skill in teaching, or is this an add-on to their regular job? If it's an add-on and they're falling behind in their own work, the result may be truncated educational sessions and frustration with the new employee. People who train others need to enjoy orienting new staff members and have instructional skills. Be realistic about the amount of time it takes to train a new person and adjust the rest of their workload accordingly.

- Adjust instructional methods. Not everyone learns the same way. If your new employee isn't catching on, the instructor (or you) may need to pivot.

- Assign a "buddy" to new workers. Managers who say they'll conduct the training often don't have time. Frequently, they aren't available to answer a new person's questions. Make sure you have a "buddy" assigned to help with time-sensitive problems and explain the mundane details a new recruit might be embarrassed to ask their boss.

- Monitor progress. Positions that are complex can require one to two (or more) years to achieve proficiency. If that's the case, establish benchmarks for three months, six months, nine months, a year, and beyond. Course corrections are needed beginning at three months (or earlier) if the staff member is lagging behind.

- Be forthright in your communication. It's much kinder to have a direct conversation than to leave your poor performer alone and hope they'll "get it." Ask how they're doing, how they feel about their progress, and whether they're having second thoughts about the job. Have you ever been in a job for which you found you really didn't have the ability? I was, and it was terrible. When I was a college student, and PDP-10s were state-of-the-art computers, I got a job as the lunchtime relief operator of a multi-college computer system. After completing the first shift, I knew I was in over my head. Consequently, I was anxious and scared each time I showed up for work. Your incompetent person may be feeling lousy too. You can be kind as you reiterate the expectations for their work performance. Hopefully, they'll have already figured out that this position isn't a good match for them (as I did) and leave for a brighter future. It's a lot easier if someone decides they want to find more suitable employment than to have to go through the process of removing them from the company.

- Be aware of your options. Your organization may, or may not, have a probationary period. Ask your human resources department. Also, laws differ state to state about whether you must "terminate for cause" or not. Again, get counsel from HR.
- Union contracts specify the exact process by which disciplinary action and termination occur.
- Consider a transfer (under certain conditions). If this person has demonstrated skills that would be better suited to another department, you might be able to facilitate a job match. This is assuming, of course, that they're an otherwise good employee. (For example, I would *not* recommend Lucinda to another department because she exhibited such poor judgment. To do so would be passing along trouble.) If you think they might succeed elsewhere, you can point them in that direction and give a heads-up to the other manager.

How to Deal with a Square Peg in a Round Hole: Advice for Coworkers

- If there's anything dangerous about what this person is doing (or not doing), let your manager know immediately. Describe the incident in detail, when it occurred, and who was there to witness it.
- If you notice they aren't catching on to the job in a reasonable period of time, provide specific observations to the lead or supervisor. "Max isn't getting it," is too general. "I've noticed that Max hasn't been able to answer basic customer questions on the phone because he continues to put them on hold and ask me," is specific.

- If you're training this person and they aren't progressing, ask them how they prefer to learn. You may need to adapt your instruction.
- If training this person was an add-on responsibility that you didn't want, or for which you don't have time, talk with your manager about reassignment to someone who enjoys it. Or negotiate what parts you keep and what you can let go.
- If you're frustrated training them, don't lash out; speak to your manager instead. Ineffective strategies: repeated tattling to the boss with the goal of getting the person fired, being critical and demeaning to the person, and gossiping to colleagues about them. Being mean-spirited sets up a nasty work environment for everyone; don't do it.

◇◇

WORKSHEET:

IF YOU THINK YOU MAY BE A SQUARE PEG IN A ROUND HOLE

Please answer the following questions with a yes or no. For each yes answer, see the advice that follows the question.

1. Are you afraid you took the wrong job?

If you're worried because you aren't catching on (and it's not because you haven't been given adequate training), perhaps you took a job for which you aren't qualified or you don't have the interest or temperament. It's miserable to be in the wrong job. I hope you'll seek other opportunities before your performance becomes such a problem that you're put on notice. Career counselors can be helpful in steering you toward positions for which you may be better suited.

2. Are you aware you took the wrong job but are hoping to deny the truth?

If you wake up dreading work each day, that may be a clue that you already know you're in the wrong job. Fear of needing to find another position can be fierce, but it'd be better if you started looking around. Flying under the radar may be giving you a paycheck for now, but eventually others will notice your lacking performance. Also, arguing with your boss, or others, to try to make yourself look more competent won't help you in the long run.

3. Have you been receiving feedback that you aren't as competent as you should be at this point in your tenure?

If you have a learning challenge or know how you learn best, be clear with those who instruct you so they can adapt teaching strategies (e.g., recorded versus written instructions, or hands-on versus lecture or online instruction). But if you're under a delusion that you're doing better than you really are, it's time to face the music even if it means you need to start job hunting again.

4. Did you take this job to get a "foot in the door" when you knew you really didn't have any interest in the position?

It's understandable to take a job to get inside an organization where you'd like to be, but you owe your current boss adequate performance at the very least. Thinking you can short-circuit doing the job you were hired to do to rapidly jump into a new position at the same company may not be realistic. Managers talk. If you can't be counted on in this job, why would any other manager in the organization want to hire you?

The Unknowing, Unskilled, and Left-to-Languish

As noted in the introduction of this chapter, there are many explanations why someone doesn't perform as well as their colleagues. One reason is that jobs morph over time. Typically, it's technology that drives work modifications. It's broken my heart to see good workers felled by a transforming environment. Perhaps training was offered to upgrade skills but it was inadequate for this person. Or the job became significantly different and they found themselves truly unqualified. Sadly, these situations more frequently happen to "mature" workers who counted on continued employment until retirement. When faced with finding a new position in their late-middle years, or beyond, they're vulnerable to age discrimination and/ or the inability to find work with the same pay and benefits.

As a consultant, I got complaints about low-performing staff members. My first question was if these hapless employees were aware of the manager's expectations. "Not in so many words," was often the answer. You need to use the words! It seemed that the longer the person was in the job, the more the boss's perspective was, "Well, they *ought* to know." But unless the manager directly spells it out, I would argue employees often *don't* know. The staff member may have gotten no or mixed messages or may have been relying on out-of-date directives.

When new leadership arrives, it's understandable the performance expectations change. However, it's unfair to label an employee incompetent if the new manager hasn't had the decency to clarify the updated measures of success. As the new supervisor, you may have been told stories about this person's stellar past performance. If you're not seeing that now, it may be your standards are different or the job requirements have changed.

You may recognize the unknowing, unskilled, and left-to-languish by some of these traits:

- They've seen bosses come and go over the years. Since they remain employed through it all (even though there may have been harsh criticism), they can become deaf to negative comments. They'll just wait out this manager too.
- They often don't understand their job is truly in jeopardy—and why would they if there have been no consequences up until now?
- They haven't been able to attain the required skill level from classes or coaching. They may not have the ability, or the training didn't work for them.

Deborah's Demise?

Deborah was proud of her thirty-two years at the company and was one of its most loyal supporters. She had certificates and pins displayed at her workstation, testament to her tenure and team spirit. Over the course of her employment, she'd held a number of non-professional jobs in almost every division. For the last seven years, she had been in the shipping and receiving department. Four years ago, technology was introduced for the logging in of packages and their delivery to their final destinations. Some packages required signatures, others did not, but each needed confirmation of delivery. Deborah was at her best with the first duties of the day, which included scanning barcodes to log the receipt of packages to the company. Unfortunately, it was not her strong suit to track the specific requirements of each package and consistently log its delivery. Most of the time this wasn't critical and wouldn't have been noticed, but on the day that a time-sensitive package went missing, she was in big trouble. It was clearly logged in to the organization but not noted as delivered—and even more importantly, to whom it was delivered.

For the eight months Deborah's manager, Tasha, had been in the position, she tried getting work-process consistency from Deborah. She hadn't succeeded. Frankly, Tasha was sick of bird-dogging Deborah's work. Then the missing package incident occurred. Tasha was called on the carpet by the vice president of her division and told to "do something about Deborah."

When Tasha came to me, the question she needed to answer was what to do about Deborah. Firing her would be a nasty move given Deborah's long tenure. And besides, Deborah had good friends in high places (other than her division's VP). To keep hounding her to do better, when she clearly couldn't, was an exercise in futility.

Tasha and I had a heart-to-heart about capitalizing on the skills Deborah *did* have. Tasha was able to rearrange the work in a manner that Deborah continued to complete the log-in of all packages and then move to the mailroom to meter afternoon mail and handle special postage issues. As a result, Deborah continued to have contact with company colleagues (which she enjoyed) and contribute where she could be successful. Fortunately, the person who'd previously been assigned to the mailroom during the afternoons was eager to be more physically active and willingly took on package delivery.

How to Deal with the Unknowing, Unskilled, and Left-to-Languish: Advice for Managers

- Give this person direct feedback about their performance in contrast to your expectations. Even if you think they should know the expectations, be clear and state them.
- Adjust instructional methods for training if they aren't catching on.
- Provide learning aids. Help them identify cues to keep them on track in the moment or if they forget and don't know what to do next.

- Build on their existing skills, talents, and abilities. They may have never been encouraged to develop in ways that are useful to the department and organization.
- Adapt duties if you can do so without causing other complications. Deborah had her duties shifted to build on what she did well and eliminate the parts she did poorly. That happy ending isn't always possible, but considering options is worthwhile. That said, be warned that adapting the job to an individual (particularly when duties are removed) can create its own problems. This can lead to inequities across a job title and may, understandably, cause resentment among other staff members.
- Retitle the job if the duties change. If you do adapt the position requirements for this person, inform yourself about the potential consequences and consider using a different job title for revised duties (but no promotion if there are fewer duties). Speak with your human resources department and/or union about whether this is an option.
- Find a better job match in a different department, assuming this is a valued staff member who's an asset to the company.
- Consider all the legal ramifications if you want to fire this person. If you decide you need to manage this person out, please contact the human resources department specifically for advice on any legal implications.

How to Deal with the Unknowing, Unskilled, and Left-to-Languish: Advice for Coworkers

- Intervene immediately to assist if something is, or isn't, happening that's dangerous. Let your boss know the details of the situation.
- Send concerns to the manager. Report (factually and without whining) your coworker's specific behaviors

regarding the task and its impact on you or customers. "Shane isn't pulling his weight," isn't specific. This is specific: "Shane promised to send the month-end numbers two days ago. I reminded him again this morning, and he said he's still not finished. As a result, I'm unable to complete the report you asked for on time."

- Know that your view may be limited. It may be tempting to keep "tattling" in the hopes that the situation will end and the person will be "terminated" (such a pretty word, yes?). Please be aware that you may not have the whole story; the boss may be doing something about this but can't say because the employee's privacy must be protected.

- Try to keep your annoyance in check. Perhaps you can share tips you've learned along the way that would help this person.

- Check in with your manager. If you've tried to help and get responses like, "I don't need to learn this," or "You're not my boss," inform your manager. Mention the reaction you've received when you provided feedback or tried to assist.

- Be polite but firm. If this coworker expects you to do their work for them, you have a perfect right to say, "No." Try not to say, "Hell no!"

◇◇

WORKSHEET:

IF YOU THINK YOU MAY BE AN UNKNOWING, UNSKILLED, AND LEFT-TO-LANGUISH

Please answer the following questions with a yes or no. For each yes answer, see the advice that follows the question.

1. Do you realize you've fallen behind?

If you're close to retirement, you have my sympathy. It's a terrible position to be in. But whether you're close to retirement or not, ignoring your skill deficits isn't helping you because it's likely your boss is well aware of the problem. If you have a decent relationship with your manager, see if you can have a heart-to-heart about the parts of the job you like and excel in and the parts that are problematic. Is there a way you can swap for other assignments? Or can you receive more individualized training? Do you need a new job altogether?

2. Are you getting feedback about lagging behind current standards?

This is a situation that will only get worse over time. Do what you can to keep up through engaging in education or training. If you really can't catch up, it's time to look at alternatives.

3. Are you asking (or worse, expecting) your colleagues to do your work for you because you're unable?

I'm sure you already know that's not fair. Get help to come up to speed or, as stated above, look at alternative employment where you can excel.

◇◇

The Infuriatingly Incompetent Boss

As a society, we're hard on managers. The cartoon Dilbert's devil-haired boss sums it up. We have high expectations and often forget that these are imperfect humans, just like the rest of us. My belief is that leadership is a calling that demands a set of skills, talents, and character traits—and not everyone is equally qualified.

I've had bosses whom I considered to be incompetent, and I've certainly gotten an earful from those who have complained to me about theirs. It's a particular challenge to deal with them because frankly, you have next to no power in the situation. As their employee, you can't fire them, and any attempt you make to try to remove your supervisor is probably not going to go well for you.

Very early in my career, I watched a drama play out between an eager mid-career chief operating officer, Brad, and the nearing-retirement president of the company. Brad had gained allies through a group of (what I consider to be) unethical consultants. Their plan was to overthrow the president by appealing to the board of trustees. Guess who lost his job? Brad, not the president.

During the ground campaign, supporters of the insurgent COO and supporters of the president publicly declared their allegiances. It was an ugly awakening for Brad's army when they needed to either pack up their rhetoric and leave or transform themselves into faithful employees of the board-approved president. Brad's cheerleaders were lucky their jobs weren't on the line as a result of what truly was insubordination.

You may have witnessed similar politics. When a popular leader is dismissed, there's sometimes a mass exodus of supporters as a statement of outrage. What's meant to send shock waves through the system, and a wake-up for radical change, typically results in little more than a small swirl before corporate life settles back into its usual rhythm.

The lesson from my early experience was to never be so naive as to think you can fire your boss. However, please don't be silent if there are illegal/fraudulent activities occurring, or if people are being abused or endangered by the action/inaction of this person. Everyone reports to someone, and it should be your prerogative to go to your boss's boss. But what could be considered "jumping the chain of command" might not feel safe in your situation. If not, talk with human resources or the union if you have one.

Register your complaints and then get on with what you *can* do. But please know that the boss you consider to be incompetent may have powerful allies. Below are some strategies that might be of help, or you may choose to leave for saner pastures.

Characteristics of Incompetent Managers

The common theme of incompetent managers is their inability to solicit or receive feedback about their style or actions that cause negative impacts to employees. Remember, many people get their management jobs as a result of superior performance in a technical role. Or promotion occurred because they've been around a long time and management was the only advancement option. They can be square pegs in round holes—in the wrong job. Or a live demonstration of the Peter Principle: promoted directly into incompetence.

Other traits of incompetent managers you might recognize:

- They exhibit an inability to focus attention on doing the work of a manager. They have more important things to do.
- They don't meet with staff members individually or collectively.
- They can't make/stick with/remember a decision.
- They inconsistently apply policies, decisions, or practices.

- They have a need to be buddies with the staff; they gossip about some workers to other workers, throw other managers under the bus, and distance themselves from "them" (upper management).
- They withhold information. Staff end up being surprised by changes that affect them.
- They aren't able to represent the department, or the staff, with any authority because their reputation is so poor in the organization.
- They play favorites or they scapegoat—or both.
- They're emotionally volatile or immature; they bleed their stress onto their staff.

The following provides three case studies of incompetent bosses, and it's an incomplete inventory. The examples are followed by suggestions for dealing with an incompetent supervisor of any stripe.

Myrna, the Unmanageable Manager

A group of three coworkers came to me about issues in their department. They cared about their work on a very personal level and had high expectations of themselves. They had a list of complaints about their boss, Myrna, whom they felt was impulsive and unaware of how her actions affected workflow. For example, she would spontaneously make assignments based on her current interests when there was no intention of using the information anytime in the foreseeable future.

As they described her, Myrna was friendly and had a ready smile. She consistently attracted highly skilled staff to her department. But once hired, the staff members were at the mercy of her inability to plan, focus, and allot time appropriately. Her mantra was, "I'm too busy right now," as she dashed off.

The specific problem that brought the three to my office was Myrna's lack of departmental planning. They never knew what was coming so they could make realistic promises to their customers. This wasn't a problem that even registered for Myrna. Her ethos was, "Burn the midnight oil!" She was energized by a crisis and took pride in her ability to pull off extraordinary measures. It never entered her mind that these crises needn't occur, that it was an inordinate burden on her staff, and (because there was never time for review) quality suffered.

By some process the three didn't understand, Myrna pulled dates out of the air thereby committing them to a schedule that was often unrealistic. Even when they pleaded, Myrna was unwilling to identify what had to happen, in what sequence, and by what date so that there was enough time for everyone to thoughtfully complete tasks. She was defensive when asked to establish priorities. The staff ended up creating their own work plans in the hope they'd be prepared to leap on the next (most likely avoidable) crisis. To add to the confusion, Myrna, who was typically hands-off, would suddenly need to have her hand in everything. Did she trust them or not?

My counsel to Myrna's staff was to be aware of what they could and couldn't control in the situation. It was likely Myrna would never be the planful manager they desired. They'd given repeated feedback and it had fallen on self-justifying ears. They might as well assume that Myrna wasn't going to change; their only hope was to change their own strategies. I suggested that they identify the pressures from above to which Myrna was subjected. The more intelligence they could gather about the demands placed on her, the better chance they had of predicting what would fall their way. On the positive side, because Myrna was more often hands-off than hands-on, they could (for the most part) operate as they wished. They agreed this was better than being micromanaged. The danger in their being so autonomous was they might not alert Myrna when they should. We discussed situations in which it would be prudent to get counsel from her since she had authority and political sway.

Explosive Evan

Evan's boss, Jason, came to me with a problem because he was out of ideas. Over the past month, he'd had an endless string of complaints about Evan, one of the managers who reported to him. It wasn't that Jason was immune to Evan's explosive temperament, but he'd assumed these were isolated stress reactions. Recently, he'd learned how frequently they occurred any time Evan received negative feedback from staff members or customers. Jason had a dilemma: he needed Evan's skill set and experience, but Evan couldn't keep behaving this way. Jason was afraid tantrums were baked into Evan's personality—which you can't change, right?

As a last-ditch effort, Jason came to see me. I asked for specifics about these outbursts. From the description, it seemed Evan was unable to regulate his anger. That's a problem for anyone, but particularly in a manager. Jason said these incidents followed a pattern and went on to describe a major eruption from the week before.

A customer asked for a variation on a standard test that Evan's group ran. When Evan came into the workroom and saw that the technician, Amanda, was making test modifications, he blew up and said she had no authority to approve changes. She should have sent the customer to him. After filleting Amanda in front of her colleagues, Evan went storming down the hall to confront the customer. He barged through the customer's door ranting, "People like you think they can go around me to get what they want!" The customer was understandably frightened. She stood up and demanded that Evan leave her office. With a shaky voice, the customer called Jason to relay the incident. Meanwhile, Evan was on the phone to human resources to complain about how badly *he* was being treated, his authority undermined at every turn.

Moments after Jason got off the phone with the customer, the technician who'd been yelled at arrived in tears. Amanda told Jason she'd had it with Evan and was ready to quit. As she described the situation, she said she had the skills and the time to revise the test per the customer's request. Weren't they exhorted to provide superior customer service? She reported that the entire team was upset, and they were at the end of their collective rope with Evan.

Amanda further explained that explosions occurred anytime Evan felt his power was threatened. The staff walked on eggshells wondering what would cause the next meltdown. Amanda said that these blowups were sometimes followed by Evan providing donuts in the breakroom. It was crazymaking. Jason listened carefully to Amanda, suggested she take the rest of the day off, and asked that she delay her decision about leaving her job. He said he would drop by the workroom to see the staff, and then would talk with Evan.

Rather predictably, Jason's meeting with Evan didn't go well. Jason reported to me that Evan felt completely justified in his reaction and dismissed the incident as "over and done with." No offer of an apology to Amanda, the customer, or the staff. The meeting ended with Jason telling Evan that this type of incident could *not* happen again, or there would be serious consequences.

After hearing the whole story, I said that I wasn't sure Evan was aware of the seriousness of the situation. He certainly discounted the degree to which he negatively impacted people. Was he so naive as to believe he could push around and scare his customers? I asked what Jason's tolerance was if there was another blowup. The answer was Evan would lose his job.

I worked with Jason on a document containing specific expectations for Evan's behavior and suggested the three of us meet. Jason would deliver the basic messages: why we were meeting, what must change, and that Evan could lose his job if there was another incident. Evan was taken aback and said that he wanted to keep his employment. I offered him coaching to assist in increasing his communication and management skills, as well as stress management techniques. The bottom line was if there were any further outbursts, Evan would be out the door. Message received.

When I worked alone with Evan, I asked him if he knew how frightening and abusive the team perceived him to be when he was "blowing off a little steam." Evan was a physically large man and surprisingly unaware of how intimidating he appeared when he was angry. Given that wasn't his intent, the door was open for change. With the details outlined for performance improvement, I initially met with him weekly to identify situations and practice alternatives so he could corral his emotional response.

Since he came from a long line of vocal, gesturing family members, volatility seemed normal to him. I video-recorded Evan while we recreated a typical situation so he could see how his choice of words, tone of voice, and body language came across. He was stunned. Now I had his attention. Going over past incidents, he was able to identify triggers to his storms. We worked on how to intervene with his thoughts and feelings *before* he went off the rails. I recommended that he offer a sincere apology to his staff (and the customer) and let them know he finally "got it" and had sought help.

Evan grew a lot over the next year. After a couple of months, our meetings became less frequent as he integrated new skills into his work life. Not everything was perfect, of course. Two of his employees were so disturbed by Evan's previous explosions they chose to leave. Eventually, he gained a degree of trust with the staff who remained, primarily by clarifying their authority for decision-making and by being more emotionally stable. He worked hard to identify patterns to his anger and found ways to avoid yelling at people by doing things such as removing himself, taking a walk, or writing down his thoughts and feelings. Sometimes he was even able to let the emotion go. He slipped up a few times, but they weren't the dramatic performances of the past and he quickly apologized.

While we continued to work together, Evan chose to regularly see a therapist. He reported that he was happier at work and his family had noticed a positive difference in him. He said he was glad, as painful as it was, that he had been given an ultimatum and had risen to the challenge.

Danielle: Unqualified, or Uncaring?

LaMar came to me for help about issues he was having with Danielle, a peer manager who was in a different reporting line. The work of their departments intersected through the hand-off of customers, which is why LaMar was talking to me. His staff members had reported that two of Danielle's employees were consistently cutting corners that could put customers at risk. The staff members had given feedback to the offending employees with no observable change as a consequence.

LaMar described the meeting he'd had with Danielle to discuss the issue and lack of improvement. It sounded like he'd provided a clear description of the problem while also giving her the benefit of the doubt about her employees' training needs. He assumed that, given the information, she would educate and coach her staff members. Her response was to repeatedly deflect and make excuses. The stakes were too high to let it go, so after having similar conversations multiple times, LaMar wanted to find a strategy that would produce a positive outcome.

I asked him who had the authority to get results from Danielle, and the answer was her boss. He decided to go through his reporting chain to alert his manager to the issues that posed potential danger to customers. His boss took the information to Danielle's manager. Whether Danielle was given the feedback by her supervisor wasn't clear because within days the inevitable happened: an error was committed by one of Danielle's staff that was so serious it had to be reported through the quality standards department.

In the face of censure from her own management and the quality council, Danielle *still* didn't own up to her staff members' performance problems. In meetings she continued to be defensive and evade responsibility. Although she was reluctant to publicly admit error, within a few weeks there were some changes. Did Danielle have such a large ego that she had to save face at all costs? Did she not know how to coach her employees? Was she ignorant, or did she not care? We'll never know. That the issues were resolved (for the moment) was enough.

This situation provided two important lessons for LaMar:

- If you've knocked on the door a couple of times regarding a serious issue and gotten no response, it's time to go to someone with more authority.
- You won't always get an apology, or even an acknowledgement of a problem, but you might see improvement. Keep your eye on the results.

How to Deal with an Incompetent Manager
- Know what's in your control and what isn't. It's tempting to think about how to get your incompetent boss fired, but you don't have the power. And your view may be limited. You're aware of how your boss negatively affects you, but you might not know how this person is valued by those above. Your manager's skill with employees may not to be the most important

factor in *their* boss's evaluation. Ultimately, it's up to their manager whether they stay or go.

- Understand that you can report your manager's incompetent behavior to their boss, but don't expect to receive progress updates. You won't be privy to any coaching or performance conversations they have.

- Try working around their incompetence by offering help in their weak areas. For example, "How would it be if I took over the calendar updates and saved you the trouble?" If you get a yes, you could have control over something that's been bothering you.

- Avoid gossiping about your manager. It's reassuring and bonding to trash-talk with colleagues. The question is, does it make any positive difference? In the moment, it might be like a piece of candy that tastes good but does nothing to ease your hunger. Spreading negativity just makes you feel worse about your job and can end up haunting you if the boss ever learns of what could be considered betrayal or even insubordination.

- Try giving specific, useful feedback to your supervisor about something that they're capable of changing. Expecting a personality transplant, or sudden expertise, isn't reasonable. A comment about the utility of having agendas for staff meetings could be. Make an offer to assist if the boss doesn't have time (or much interest).

- Do an assessment of the trade-offs in your job: what's positive, what's negative. If the balance is toward the positive, you can probably live with your incompetent boss. Remind yourself that no job (or boss) is perfect. Focusing on what you really enjoy about your work can increase your job satisfaction and perspective.

- Consider all your options. If the situation with your manager is getting to the point that you're doing unhealthy things to soothe yourself, it may be time to consider leaving. If you must stay, work on coping strategies that don't make you sick, an insomniac, or a constant whiner.

- Be realistic. There have been times in my life that I've done work I didn't enjoy, for people I didn't like, and yet been extremely grateful for the paycheck. If this applies to you, please take stock of what you *do* get from the job so you can stay motivated. Of course, you're in a better position to be picky about your job (and boss) when your financial situation is stable.

- Report the "Despicables." I won't take much time on the worst of the worst. The answer of what to do is clear: report them. These are the supervisors who have a case of the "-ists" (racist, sexist, ageist, or fill in the blank of some other ignorant intolerance). These disgraceful behaviors are illegal if they affect your employment. If you are subjected to any of them, contact your human resources department, your boss's boss, the Equal Employment Opportunity Commission (EEOC), the union, or whomever else it makes sense to alert. If you believe it's unsafe for you to make a report, please consider whether you can afford to stay under these conditions. Standing by and doing nothing has its own risks.

◇◇

WORKSHEET:
IF YOU THINK YOU MAY BE AN
INCOMPETENT MANAGER

Please answer the following questions with a yes or no. For each yes answer, see the advice that follows the question.

1. Have you been receiving complaints from human resources or your boss about how you manage people?

It can be embarrassing to be called out and you may be feeling ashamed. But these emotions may keep you from looking at the situation with clear eyes. Take complaints seriously and seek guidance through coaching and/or leadership classes.

2. Do you ignore feedback from your staff about how your actions negatively impact them?

If you've been telling yourself that employees are never happy as an excuse for not hearing what they're telling you, that's a mistake. A one-off complaint is one thing, but if there are multiple people complaining about the same thing, it's time to pay attention. How can your people do their best work and make you and the department look good if you engage in actions that undermine them?

3. Are you in a management-level job because it was the only way to "move up" and receive more money and/or prestige?

If you don't really have a passion to be of service to others as their supervisor or leader, then I'd question whether you're in the right job. You may be better off as an individual contributor rather than leading others.

4. Do you resonate with the case study of Evan (the emotionally volatile manager)?

This is very serious business. Anyone might blow up on a *rare* occasion, but repeated emotional outbursts (whether followed by an apology or not) is abuse. You hold people hostage by your emotional unpredictability, and you can't pay people enough to make up for it. This type of behavior leads to complaints of a hostile workplace and could get you in big and expensive trouble. Even though you may be resistant (or think *you* are the victim in the situation), I highly recommend that you seek the assistance of a therapist or a coach. It's possible to learn new strategies, but the key is that you must want different results and put in the effort to get there. If you choose this path, I applaud you for your bravery in examining, *and changing*, patterns of damaging behavior. The consequences can positively impact your life and career.

<><><><><><><><><><><><><><><><><><><><><><><><><><><><><><><><><><><><>

Summary for Dealing with Any Incompetent Jerk

- Examine your own motives. Is the person truly incompetent, or do you not like them and want them gone? If that's the case, then deal with your emotions but don't try to push someone out by labeling them incompetent.
- Make a realistic assessment regarding the degree of control you actually have in the situation. What you always have control over are *your* actions and reactions. Unless you are that person's boss, you don't have the authority to fire them.
- Have some empathy for the person who's struggling. Give feedback and/or offer help; don't gossip behind their back. It's not helpful and often causes more damage.

- Tell someone who is able to make a difference. If the incompetent's actions (or lack of action) are dangerous, illegal, fraudulent, or costly, you need to take action by alerting those with authority.
- Do what you can to make a positive difference but know where the line is that signals it's time to get out. An incompetent colleague may be easier to bear than an incompetent boss, but if the situation becomes intolerable, it's time to consider other employment options.

Chapter Five:

THE RUNAWAY-TRAIN JERK

Runaway trains can't stop and are a danger to everyone and everything in their destructive path. The commonality among the Runaway-Train Jerks are their excessiveness; they have trouble adjusting their speed and direction. When the less extreme version of themselves emerges, many of them are tolerable, and even valued, colleagues. It's the radical nature of each that can drive you batty.

In this chapter, we'll cover:

- **The High-Speed Train** (can't slow down to include you)
- **The Funeral Train** (everything is terrible)
- **The Hazardous Materials Train** (truly bad behavior)
- **The Milk-Run Train** (very slow . . .)
- **The Stop-at-All-Crossings Train** (detailed to a fault)
- **The Circuitous Train** (the indirect communicator)

The High-Speed Train

These are people who have a lot to accomplish and woe be it to those who get in their way! In fairness, they produce. The quality, however, isn't always as spot-on as it could be because they tend to do everything on their own—and rapidly.

Their mantra is, "It needs to get done *now*; we can always make changes later." As any list maker knows, there's a lot of satisfaction in crossing off items. However, it's a problem when productivity overrules all other considerations.

Some of their telling characteristics include:

- They assume that if you have something to say, you'll speak up. Silence, to them, is agreement. They don't tend to look around and ask, "What do you think?" or read the subtleties of body language that indicate disagreement. Nor do they give you time to respond to their email or texted ideas before they assume you concur.
- They exhibit a lack of graciousness in accepting others' ideas, especially criticism. You're likely to get an argument or defensiveness. However, their response may moderate upon reflection.
- They show anxiety when no one is in charge or they perceive a void in leadership—which can make them a real challenge to their manager. They have little hesitation to step in and take over.
- They have an ability to wade into clashes. Since they're less sensitive to conflict, they don't understand why others are reluctant to engage in its resolution.
- They engage in behaviors like being pushy and controlling. It doesn't occur to them how they affect others (of if it does, they may not care).
- They value being highly productive. They're ready to set direction and contribute. They may possess great dedication to the organization's mission even if they're tough with their colleagues.

Chuck's Challenge

A friend of mine who was a mid-manager in a public agency, Chuck, contacted me to conduct a staff team-building session using a personality profile. He wanted his staff to talk about their commonalities and differences and hoped for increased tolerance among them. As we were winding up the conversation, he causally said, "I should tell you that there's this person . . ." Ah, yes, *this person.*

In about 90 percent of the groups with whom I have worked, the "identified patient" in any team was a Runaway-Train type, usually a High-Speed Train. They move at a clip that leaves no room for conversation or collaboration. They have a destination to which they are hurtling, and people can be struck by a moving train.

The woman in question, Bette, was on a mission. She came into the office with blinders on, probably because she was mentally at work as soon as her eyes opened in the morning. Each day, she barreled past a group of colleagues without any acknowledgement that they were breathing the same air. She'd slap her things onto her desk and get on the job—leaving a host of people wondering what they did wrong since Bette had rudely dashed past them without even a glance.

At the workshop, there were no surprises in the group's scores. Bette was the lone person on the high-assertive/low-relationship side—but I'd never seen anyone with such a high score. No doubt she believed she fit this category, but a super high score often indicates the person values these characteristics as well ("Everyone could be a little more like me").

I spoke with the group about adapting their styles to communicate more effectively with each other and offered the suggestion of saying good morning to colleagues as an example of how to flex a low-relationship style. At the break, Bette flew to me bristling with anger saying she couldn't believe I would expect her to actually say good morning to people. I asked her if she thought it would take too much time. "Of course it would!" she snapped. I suggested she could look at people and say good morning *while* she continued to walk (not run) to her cube.

Years later, I learned that Bette moved to Hawaii. Living on island time? I always wondered how that worked out.

How to Deal with a High-Speed Train

- Know your audience! If you want them to slow down, you need to appeal to their needs for efficiency and expediency. For example, "If you ask for input now, it'll save time because you won't have to go through this again."
- Use thinking language instead of feeling language. Say, "We need to know the information is correct before proceeding," instead of, "I feel like you're driving so hard that we can't be accurate."
- Don't take pushback personally if you deliver criticism. Give them time to reflect, then see what changes. The proof is in their actions, not what they say.
- Assert yourself more than normal when necessary. A High-Speed Train can run straight past flashing lights and downed rail crossings. If you see a car on the tracks and assume your cry of impending disaster will get their attention, it might not. Pump it up: "STOP! I need you to hear this!"
- Get to the point. Their tolerance for "fluff" is low. And pretty much anything beyond, "How are you today?" (which they may not feel obligated to answer) is fluff in their estimation.
- Read their cues to assess the amount of socializing they can tolerate. Many High-Speed Trains aren't as extreme as Bette; they may show more desire for social interaction. The School of Hard Knocks may have taught them to involve others. Even so, their default mode is getting it done—with or without you.

- Let them know why you want to talk and about how long it will take. If you need something from them, remember they value their time and productivity. Their anxiety goes up if they're worried you'll talk too long or they think it's a waste of time.

<><><><><><><><><><><><><><><><><><><><><><><><><><><><><><><><><><><><><><>

WORKSHEET:
IF YOU THINK YOU MAY BE A HIGH-SPEED TRAIN

Please answer the following questions with a yes or no. For each yes answer, see the advice that follows the question.

1.Does your pace energize you but exhaust others?
Beware of discounting those who want to slow down or be more cautious. Take a moment, ask questions, and listen to the answers. You have something to learn from them.

2. Are you aware of what types of situations cause you anxiety?
Become familiar with (and apply) techniques that slow down your racing brain. Frenetic action may be your way of trying to manage stress. Meditation and/or learning to change your internal dialogue may be a good practice for you. Say things to yourself like, "Breathe and settle down a minute." This might help you reduce the chatter in your head that compels you to keep going even faster.

3. Does it bother you when others don't step up to conflict challenges?
You probably think everyone is wired the way you are, but rest assured they aren't. Being able to address conflict is a

strength of yours. You may or may not enjoy it, but you certainly aren't afraid of it like some.

4. Are you unable to get the results you want from colleagues?
Asking (not demanding) that others partner with you could result in better results than going it alone—or being in the position where you push them to do things your way.

∞∞∞

The Funeral Train

I grew up around a Funeral Train relative. When she was on a roll, her glass was not only half-empty, there was scum on the bottom. If I tried to counter, the response I got was, "I'm a realist," as if anyone who wasn't pessimistic was living in a fantasy world. A. A. Milne's Winnie-the-Pooh character Eeyore comes to mind: "End of the road. Nothing to do, and no hope of things getting better."

I've engaged in my share of negativity over the years, as I'm sure friends and colleagues would attest. If you've got that propensity to begin with, it's easy to slip into. No doubt we were wired with the survival mechanism to notice what's wrong or dangerous to keep the species alive. However, if you're like me with a shakier grip on a glass half-full than you'd like, a constant stream of defeatist comments ups your stress and drags you down.

You might recognize the Funeral Train by the following:

- They often have enough facts woven into their negative prognostications that you can't ignore them altogether.
- They can, unfortunately, easily switch from "what's wrong" to "who's wrong."
- They need to be in the know and hate to be surprised. That's why they have so many versions of doom and gloom—nothing will surprise them!

95

- They're sometimes right, which only reinforces their belief that they're accurate about what will go wrong in any situation.
- They have unflattering names for those with sunnier dispositions. They believe those people aren't in touch with reality.
- They may have observations worth listening to, but the packaging is lousy.

Oksana's Options

Oksana was the supervisor of a department that packaged a variety of small tools and equipment for delivery. Her employees' work was rote, comprised of sorting, packing, labeling, and delivery. Her manager suggested Oksana meet with me for management advice.

Oksana's story contained as many issues as the eight people in her department. Among them were lack of skill/inconsistent work, emotional regulation problems of staff members that led to volatile interactions, physical differences that prompted arguments about job equity, and a generalized negative outlook that spread like wildfire if any one of them started to complain.

Oksana told me that her employees were protected by upper management and that dismissal of any of them wasn't an option—even though it seemed to me Oksana wanted to fire them all. I asked how she communicated her performance expectations. The answer: she didn't. They had a job description—what more did they need?

The first crew member arrived ninety minutes before Oksana did, so they were on their own. I asked if she had a "huddle" in the morning once everyone was present so they could go over the work for the day, set priorities, and create a positive tone for teamwork. Not possible, she said. They were already dispersed by the time Oksana got there; she wasn't going to gather them.

You're probably wondering if Oksana could come to work earlier. You'd be correct if you guessed her answer was no.

I asked if, upon her arrival, Oksana toured the floor to coach those who needed help, provide praise for good work, or intervene if skirmishes occurred. Nope. She was at the computer in another room—doing what was never clear. I asked if she'd tried having staff meetings and introducing fun challenges to promote teamwork. She was sure they wouldn't do it.

I met with Oksana three times. At each session, I suggested different strategies to get her engaged in doing *something* to make things better. She offered her own suggestion: I could show up at the beginning of the shift (when she wasn't there) and "talk to them." No, I wasn't going to manage her staff for her.

I'm not the right coach if after three sessions things aren't improving. Oksana had enjoyed a change of scenery by coming to my office, but she wanted magic—to get different results by doing nothing different. We stopped meeting.

How to Deal with a Funeral Train

- Stop debating. Arguing with their negative outlook isn't going to get you anywhere. If you have direct evidence to the contrary, feel free to present it. Their response may well be, "Maybe this time—but next time watch out!"
- Listen carefully for the content above and beyond the negative tone. Is there something important in their message? It's easy to ignore people who are consistently bleak and then end up missing a real nugget of information.
- Try giving direct feedback. If you have an otherwise good relationship with this person, let them know how their negativity bothers you. You might say something

like, "I'm sure you don't intend this, but your gloomy comments really bring me down. I wonder if you could do less of that around me," (i.e., Might you suffer in silence?).

- Look for patterns. Are there situations that produce a stream of fatalism? If so, you might say something like, "I notice that you get into a negative spin each time the project is mentioned. What's up?"
- Redirect the conversation. Switch the topic or don't respond to the doom and gloom.
- Stop fighting what you can't change. As with so many irritating behaviors, you may have to let this roll off you. Establishing an internal monologue of, "That's just Oksana," or "Breathe and let it go!" can be your stress mantra.
- Put the ball in their court. If you manage a person who always has a complaint about the department/colleagues/the work/you, try the well-tested intervention of asking them to come up with a proposal of how to make things better. This will put the kibosh on their comments if they just wanted to whine. Otherwise, you'll have ideas from a person who could be invested in creating improvements.
- Stop the interaction. If all else fails, you could do what a friend of mine did to me (after I shot down all *her* good advice): "Well, I guess you'd know." Then walk away.

◇◇

WORKSHEET:
IF YOU THINK YOU MAY BE A FUNERAL TRAIN

Please answer the following questions with a yes or no. For each yes answer, see the advice that follows the question.

1. Do you use negative statements as a way to gain colleagues' interest and participation in problem-solving?
Negativity is demotivating to a lot of people. Try using questions like, "How do you think we might reduce our turn-around time?" rather than a negative statement like, "Our customers are continuing to complain."

2. Do you always bring up what won't work when others are offering solutions?
Try suggesting that they look at both pros and cons instead. That way you might have an easier time discussing the negatives of a proposed solution and you might become aware of positives you hadn't considered.

3. Do you shoot down coworkers' ideas?
Nothing will tank an enthusiastic idea-generating person faster than a stick-in-the-mud who finds fault with every possibility. Add value by building on their ideas.

4. Do you consider yourself the "devil's advocate"?
Be aware that this can be an excuse for being critical and not listening carefully to ideas with potential.

5. Do you label others as "out of touch with reality" if they are positive in their outlook?

One can have a realistic view of the world and still be a happy and upbeat person.

6. Do you have a reluctance to take action to make things better?

If so, that's where you need to focus. Don't be like Oksana who was unable to get off the dime and do anything because she saw herself as a victim and was unwilling to change.

7. Do you consider yourself to be a glass half-empty person?

There are a variety of things that might help if you're interested in noticing more positives. One is to tune into your negative thoughts and challenge them. For example, a thought of, "There's never enough time to get these assignments done," could be challenged with, "I've been able to complete assignments on time even with constraints." Another strategy is to give yourself the daily homework of noticing three good things that happened at work and writing them down. For bonus points, you might include who was involved in each, as well as your own contributions.

◇◇

The Hazardous Materials Train

These folks leak toxic fumes wherever they go. In contrast to the negative comments described in the Funeral Train, they distribute harsh, unrelenting criticism—and meanness. They have a talent for finding your soft spot, then pounding on it.

They can be quite aware of their negative impact on others but enjoy the reactions of fear or submission that they receive.

Telltale signs you've met one of them:

- They leak toxicity through muttered, hurtful words, like, "No one around here knows what they're doing,"

100

or "Do I have to do everything?" as if those in proximity (typically their intended targets) can't hear.

- They may engage in emotional outbursts: screaming, crying, throwing things, and/or swearing.
- They may be just as happy to have people fear them; it gives them a feeling of power.

Bombardier Ben

Early in my consulting practice, I was eager and excited— and desperate for work! I received a call from an established consultant who wanted to discuss a potential subcontract arrangement with a multinational client. I met Ben for lunch and was put under the microscope about my skills. I passed muster and I was asked to accompany him and his associate, Silvie, on two out-of-state trips. Ben and Silvie would conduct the training; I was to document and produce an instructor's manual. If he approved my work, and the client liked me, I would eventually conduct the training myself. A red flag went up when Ben asked if I was wearing my best clothes that day because if so, I needed to upscale my wardrobe.

The two trips were horrific. The man had to be in control of everything and everyone. He created chaos wherever he went. Without my consent, he ordered my food on the plane to mirror his own special order. Ben told us when we were rising in the morning, going to the gym, and eating meals. He performed beautifully in front of the group; then at dinner he'd trash-talk the client. I was having second thoughts about continuing this work, even with meager funds in the bank.

On the way home from the second trip, Ben started a fight at the airport check-in counter (over what, I don't recall). He next berated two female flight attendants in the first-class section where we were seated. These women, who've regularly dealt with every sort of appalling behavior, were in tears. Silvie, accustomed to the role of peacemaker (read:

enabler), stepped in and calmed the waters. Again and again, she intervened during the four-hour trip. Mortified by the entire episode, I ordered a drink, put on headphones, and couldn't wait for the plane to land.

Within weeks, I completed and submitted the instructor's manual. I had fulfilled the agreement. The next month, I was on the short list to receive a three-year training contract with a local institution. I was overjoyed! It was interesting work and offered a degree of financial security. The next training event for Ben's client was more than six months out and he was in receipt of the promised document. I sent him written notice that due to my large contract, I would need to bow out; he had the training materials in hand and sufficient time to find another trainer.

The threatening letter I received in return said he would sue me for breach of contract unless I went on the next trip. The reality was that there was no contract, only the initial agreement that I'd completed. But the threat terrified me! I had no money, was new to business, and didn't know what he might do to my reputation. I went down a treacherous path of "what-ifs" in my head. The only way I knew to deal with a bully was to fight back. I wrote a letter that was sent on a friend-of-a-friend's law firm letterhead to give it some punch. Ben, of course, needed the last word via one more vitriolic letter. I didn't respond.

After I was an established consultant, I ran into Ben at a meeting. The giant monster I'd built up in my mind turned out to be a rather scrawny guy. Fear is great for producing overblown images.

How to Deal with a Hazardous Materials Train
- For managers/supervisors: Wise up and performance-manage this hazardous person up or out! Get help from HR on what you need to do. I've seen entire departments

held hostage to one person's outrageous outbursts. In these cases, the manager (when confronted about why this person is still employed) often says, "But they're the only one who has these skills." Believe me, someone else in the workforce has this proficiency. The damage caused by keeping them around is far more serious than you want to believe.

- For coworkers: Start with your boss to report a coworker's bullying. If you get no response, go to human resources. Consider your options if nothing changes.

- For coworkers or subordinates: Take care of yourself. Depending on your background, a coworker's pushy or abusive behavior (including inappropriate texts or emails) can leave you feeling extremely unsafe, even more so if it's your manager. If the boss is the problem, alert someone who has more authority (e.g., their boss, HR, the union, etc.). If you feel talking to someone in authority isn't safe for you, ask yourself whether you can thrive in this environment—or whether you need to get out.

<><><><><><><><><><><><><><><><><><><><><><><><><><><><><><><>

WORKSHEET:

IF YOU THINK YOU MAY BE A HAZARDOUS

MATERIALS TRAIN

Please answer the following questions with a yes or no. For each yes answer, see the advice that follows the question.

1. Have you been told you're controlling?

It's a very slippery slope toward narcissism if you decide you need to be in charge of everyone and everything, and believe your judgment is best. Please see the section on Narcissistic Leaders from Chapter Two and consider seeing a therapist.

2. Do you make nasty and critical comments for the express purpose of hurting people or to get things from them? Do you troll people?

I won't mince words: this is abusive, bullying behavior and can get you into big trouble. If you can't stop this behavior on your own, you might want to seek help from a therapist. If you're the leader, be aware your staff will put in more effort if you respect them and treat them well. Nasty comments lead to less productivity, gossip, people getting sick or taking mental health days, and/or purposely slowing down. Seek help from a leadership coach on the role of a leader and how to motivate others.

3. Do you have trouble controlling your temper?

If you're creating episodes worthy of an opera to get your way or deflecting responsibility, that's not efficient or effective in the long run. You might get a quick win, but people are wondering how to get you out the door. You may need to learn how to state your wants and needs without being angry or dramatic. Coaches and counselors can help. I'm sure these episodes are exhausting for you, and they're awful for those around you.

<><><><><><><><><><><><><><><><><><><><><><><><><><><><><><><><><><><><>

The Milk-Run Train

Milk runs were trains that stopped at numerous dairy farms to pick up and deliver products. They also transported people. This was a way that neighbors could visit and, given the slow transit, engage in local gossip. In contrast to the High-Speed Train, which we might consider to be an "express," the Milk Run is the "local"—making stop after stop before completing its circuit.

People who have a gift for socializing can take up an astonishing amount of time during the day checking in with people. While building relationships often pays off in getting work accomplished through others, it takes time away from the completion of one's individual tasks. Waiting for a social connector to pay attention to the mundane work at hand can slow everything up. Yet their networks and contacts may be advantageous, not just for themselves but for the company.

However, an extreme version of a Milk-Run Train colleague can be frustrating, especially if you're the one picking up the slack.

How you might recognize the Milk-Run Train:

- They have multiple groups of friends and associates and use those contacts to conduct business. You want them on your team if you need donations for an event!
- They spend a lot of time on social media or calls that may have nothing to do with their work.
- They make friends easily and tend to remember details about people as a sign of their bond.
- They may, or may not, be fulfilling their work obligations. But that's between their manager and them.

Sabrina, the Social Connector

Raoul came to me after class to ask for some advice about dealing with his colleague and next-door cubemate, Sabrina. He liked Sabrina—and who wouldn't? She was friendly, upbeat, interested in others, and connected people with common work and personal interests. While she put a lot of attention into building and nurturing communities, she wasn't nearly as mindful of fulfilling her own duties.

Raoul maintained a healthy "none of my business" attitude and figured their manager would notice and speak to her. Nothing changed. Raoul found himself increasingly impacted by Sabrina's clients calling him, or showing up at his cube, because they couldn't find her and she wasn't timely in responding to texts or emails. Sometimes they left detailed messages for him to pass along. Raoul dutifully relayed these missives to Sabrina, who was thankful to receive them—then she wandered off again. Raoul was tired of being Sabrina's assistant.

Additionally, it stuck in Raoul's craw that Sabrina wasn't demonstrating his idea of a good work ethic. In his estimation, she was goofing off and getting paid for it. We talked about how his values were affronted by Sabrina's socializing and it was only making him angrier. He could talk himself down by either repeating his mantra of, "None of my business," or finding another one like, "That's just Sabrina." We discussed setting appropriate boundaries regarding communiqués to her that he felt obliged to deliver.

I mentioned it was possible that Sabrina wasn't aware of how disruptive her stream of visitors was for Raoul. He could let her know by saying something like, "Sabrina, a number of people come by each day and interrupt me because they can't find you. Would you be able to post something on your cube that indicates when you'll be back? Please leave some paper so people can write you a note, or your number so they can text."

A month later, I saw Raoul and asked how things were going. He said he'd had the conversation with Sabrina and it went well. She was embarrassed his work had been disrupted on her behalf. She'd done what he suggested, and on her posted "due back" note she added, "Please don't disturb Raoul."

How to Deal with a Milk-Run Train

- State clearly you can't do their work. Rather than just stopping and hoping they'll notice (that's passive-aggressive), tell them you can't continue doing their tasks as well as your own.

- Set boundaries. If you (like Raoul) are being bothered by people looking for them or asking you to deliver messages, let your social connector colleague know it's inconvenient and ask that they make other arrangements.
- Ask them for help if there's something you need. Often they're generous people who will gladly share their contacts or make an introduction.
- Look for their positive contributions, even if it's not what you think they should be doing.
- Ask for help. If you've spoken to your social connector but you're still picking up their work, speak with your manager.
- Managers, play to their strengths. If you're this person's supervisor, by now you've probably realized that detail work is not their sweet spot. They're best placed in positions that use their talents for building connections, such as community outreach or representing the company at industry fairs. Rather than being frustrated by their lack of ability in a job for which they aren't suited, help them recognize where their passion lies and support their efforts to find the right job. You may have to push them out of the nest if they can't meet the expectations of their current role. Continuing to harangue them to change when they can't isn't helpful to anyone. (See the "Square Peg in a Round Hole" section of the Incompetent Jerk chapter.)

<><><><><><><><><><><><><><><><><><><><><><><><><><><><><><><><><><><><>

WORKSHEET:
IF YOU THINK YOU MAY BE A MILK-RUN TRAIN

Please answer the following questions with a yes or no. For each yes answer, see the advice that follows the question.

1. Do people think you're goofing off at work?
That's what it looks like if you're socializing excessively. If it's part of your job, help others understand what you're doing and why. Hopefully, your title reflects something about community relations. If you are actually goofing off as a way to avoid work, you may not be in the right job.

2. Are you building networks when it's not your job?
Balance your calling with the work you're assigned to do if that's the job you want to keep. Otherwise, look for another position that capitalizes on your talents for bringing people together.

<><><><><><><><><><><><><><><><><><><><><><><><><><><><><><><><><><><><>

The Stop-at-All-Crossings Train
An extremely detailed person can slow up work by diving into the minutiae of an issue, wasting time digging further and further into (what appears to be) unneeded research. Yet their diligence may inform better decisions. Their need to question, slow down the process, and research to the point they're satisfied can hold up work and make tempers flare.

You may recognize them by:

- A never-ending desire for perfection—which slows up everything.

- Analysis paralysis: They can't make a decision because there are too many factors to consider.
- Extreme detail in their work, even when it's not required.
- Anxiety over changes.
- Desire to have everything spelled out, contingency plans, and assurances.

In-the-Weeds Will

Phuong came to me about one of her employees, Will. Since they were a financial department, everyone possessed an analytical streak. The problem was how detailed Will was, the length of time it took him to complete his work, and his excessively long emails with never-ending questions. Even Will's lengthy conversational pauses were enough to get on Phuong's nerves. She was a bit of a High-Speed Train and wanted to scream at him, "Spit it out!"

I asked Phuong what feedback she'd given Will. It amounted to, "Please, speed it up," and "I don't have time to go through all these emails from you." I asked how he responded. She thought he'd gotten even slower, and he continued to send lengthy emails. How was the quality of his work? Excellent. Phuong went on to give an example. She'd asked Will to identify and compare daily ledger software packages and make a recommendation. That was over a month ago. I asked if she'd given him a deadline. No. When she recently asked him about it, Will said since he hadn't gotten a response to his emails about the parameters of the assignment (which he felt were too vague), he'd created his own parameters. He'd established ten criteria and was comparing five vendors, creating a spreadsheet with the results. He was about 80 percent done. Phuong told me she was exasperated. It was a relatively simple assignment, and he'd turned it into a big deal. Her comment was that this was a minor purchase—at this point she wondered how many dollars in wages had been spent.

I suggested to Phuong that her instructions be much more specific and include deadlines as well as at least one check-in on progress partway through.

Will wasn't trying to be annoying; he was doing it "right" to meet his quality standards. To get a better idea of how he would approach a project, she needed to have him explain his plan before he started and answer an agreed-upon number of emails he'd inevitably follow up with. If she had concerns about him going down rabbit holes of research, she could stop him early in the process. Given that Phuong's deadlines would always feel like too much pressure to Will, she needed to let him know she had his back if he was worried about cutting corners. People who are that analytical tend to have a low tolerance for risk.

Phuong let the ledger project grind to its inevitable conclusion but used the new strategy for the next assignment. When I saw her a few months later, she reported that being more specific with Will and answering more of his questions up front benefited them both. When he pushed back on some of the processes she wanted him to use (that he felt were inadequate), she gained clarity and understanding about his concerns and found some of them to be legitimate. They compromised more. Will was less reluctant to show Phuong his draft work since he was now confident they would discuss it. She reported that he was speaking up more and not sending as many emails. She was working on patience: biting her tongue and not interrupting to give Will time to get his thoughts out.

How to Deal with a Stop-at-All-Crossings Train: Advice for Managers

- Slow down and take the time to answer their questions at the beginning of a project. This may limit the number of emails you receive asking for clarification. You may be tempted to make unflattering (and quite possibly wrong) assumptions about their desire to do the work because of their numerous queries. Their motive is to obtain information about the assignment that, from their perspective, allows them to do the job properly. Your impatience only reinforces their concern that the assignment hasn't been well thought out and will result in substandard work.

- Give them the benefit of the doubt. Because their analytical brain naturally goes down a path of "what if" you may assume that they are being negative when, in fact, they're attempting to understand and plan.
- Be clear about scope and deadlines. You may need to negotiate the terms of the assignment, the level of detail and/or analysis. This may be a two (or three)-part conversation as they're likely to have additional questions once they think about it.
- Use their talents in ways that benefit the company and them. These people do their best under conditions that are more predictable, have less time pressure, and consist of work that requires detail and thoroughness. They like having a set of protocols or decision trees to fall back on.

How to Deal with a Stop-at-All-Crossings Train: Advice for Coworkers

- Understand your differences and your role. If you are a high-volume producer, the pace of a Will can drive you over the edge. But unless you're their supervisor, how much they produce isn't your business.
- Let them do their own work. Picking up the slack will only make you resentful. If there's an expectation by your Stop-at-All-Crossings Train that you'll do some of their work, say no (unless you can make a mutually beneficial trade).

- Realize that you may benefit from their detailed nature. Ask for their advice, particularly for anything that requires careful consideration of pros and cons. That's their specialty.

⸮⸮⸮⸮⸮⸮⸮⸮⸮⸮⸮⸮⸮⸮⸮⸮⸮⸮⸮⸮⸮⸮⸮⸮⸮⸮⸮⸮⸮⸮⸮⸮⸮

WORKSHEET:
IF YOU THINK YOU MAY BE A
STOP-AT-ALL-CROSSINGS TRAIN

Please answer the following questions with a yes or no. For each yes answer, see the advice that follows the question.

1. Do people complain that you hold them up by your need for excessive thoroughness?
Be mindful of how your pace affects others' work. While you may frequently feel pushed to do things faster than you believe is prudent, others wonder why you can't speed up.

2. Do you inundate your boss and others with emails filled with the details of your actions and/or long lists of questions? Is this because you're actually looking for reassurance or praise rather than information?
Be honest with yourself about whether you're looking for attention or really have important questions needing answers. If you want reassurance from your manager about the quality of your work, or assurance you're doing what was requested, ask for regular update meetings. Go prepared with a short, succinct list and up to a few important questions that you need answered. Writing long emails may be considered wasted time by your manager, and folks are probably tired of reading and responding to them (if they

respond at all). If what you're looking for is compliments, give yourself praise and tell a family member or friend who can pat you on the back.

3. Do you worry about meeting a set of standards that others might not share?

Have a conversation with your boss about what's acceptable. You may be striving for a level of perfection that isn't reasonable, or even desired.

4. Do you worry that you're not in the right job?

You're likely to do better in one that has rules, procedures, and time to think than in a position that requires you to be spontaneous and improvise as you go along.

◇◇

The Circuitous Train

Our communication varies in its assertiveness, the degree to which we clearly articulate our wants and needs. Much of this is cultural: family, community, region, and country of origin. US business communication (standards set by white men) is more assertive/direct than in many other countries. When I've worked with people from cultures that use an indirect communication style, our lack of ability to understand contextual communication is often confounding to them.

For example, we don't read the subtleties of the word "yes," as they do in some cultures. As a result we don't know how to assess their response as a promise (yes), an "I'll try," or a "no." Given that most of us work in a multicultural workforce (and/or with worldwide partners), we need to be alert to how our communication is received and understood, and adjust accordingly.

As a direct communicator, I just spit it out. As a result of being assertive, there have been times I've been judged as rude. One can, of course, be direct *and* polite. It's a matter of choosing your words and keeping out of the blame game.

Others, by nature or culture, are less assertive and more indirect in their communication. They use moderating words and hints that are meant to be discerned and acted upon. A direct communicator can miss the point altogether. I know that when someone is disappointed or angry that I didn't receive and act on a veiled request, I'm taken by surprise and impatiently wonder, "Why didn't you just tell me?"

If a direct communicator is blunt (to the point of being an instrument of destruction), their task is to tone it down and be gentler.

Indirect communicators, who go through a circuitous route to get to the point, are our focus here.

You may recognize characteristics of the Circuitous Train:

- They expect a degree of mind reading from others ("If you loved me, you'd know what I'm thinking") or that you should understand the nuances of their voice tone or body language.
- They have a special lingo with the people they are closest to that not everyone would know or understand. It doesn't occur to them that you might not get it.
- They think that hinting or speaking vaguely about what might happen is sufficient to get your attention. An example of indirect language to request you use less cream: "I suppose I could go to the store and get more cream . . ." Direct language is: "There's not much cream, would you leave some for me?"
- They may use a dangling statement with the expectation that you'll fill in the missing words by volunteering

to do something. For example, "I noticed we're out of paper in the printer . . ." Perhaps they think that if they don't ask outright, there's less risk you'll say no.

Read-My-Mind Rita

Rita came to me for some advice about how to deal with her manager, Antonia. She felt that she was unfairly burdened with extra work while a colleague, Samara, was out on maternity leave. Rita was doing her own job plus covering Samara's desk for issues that needed immediate attention. I asked if anyone else was helping out. She said no, so I inquired how this inequity came about. Rita said her boss had asked if anyone in the group would be willing to pitch in while Samara was out for three months. Rita volunteered; no one else did. I replied, "You offered and were willing, right? What changed?"

Rita didn't expect it would be so much work. She also thought that by doing a favor for her boss, she'd receive some recognition, and maybe additional compensation, or future promotion.

It seemed to me that this was a case of dashed (and unstated) expectations. I asked Rita if she'd spoken to Antonia about relieving her of the additional assignment. The answer was no. She had a lot of justifications for why it wasn't okay to speak up: she liked Samara and wanted to be helpful, Antonia might not think she was a team player, she didn't want to disappoint Antonia by going back on her word, she didn't have the courage to speak up, etc. When I asked Rita how Antonia was supposed to know that she was unhappy with the current arrangement, she said, "Well, when she asked me to look up some numbers for her, I told her I didn't have time and I wasn't very nice about it. I thought she'd realize I was overworked." When I asked what "not being very nice" sounded like, she said she'd used a "snippy" tone of voice.

I suggested Antonia was probably focused on getting her number request resolved. Expecting her to understand that a snarky tone and "I don't have time" was a cue to ask, "Are you overly burdened by helping with Samara's desk?" wasn't reasonable. I asked Rita if she thought she could approach her boss to explain that she was feeling burned out by the extra work and ask for what she wanted. It turned out Rita wasn't sure what she wanted from Antonia.

I find that people often know what they *don't* want but have trouble stating what they *do* want. Upon reflection, Rita said she wanted to reduce the extra work by half, have someone else pick up the rest, and receive some form of compensation for the additional effort she had been putting in. I asked what she thought was a reasonable reward. Sponsored attendance at a local conference was the response. It sounded like Rita had a plan. We practiced saying the words a few times until she felt confident in her ability to speak to Antonia.

A couple of days later, I got an email from Rita saying that Antonia had been very responsive to her request to cut down the extra work and attend a conference. Antonia said she was grateful for the extra help Rita had provided. Her only additional comment was, "Why didn't you tell me sooner that you were feeling burned out?"

How to Deal with a Circuitous Train

- Clarify the communication assumptions. If you learn that a Rita is disappointed by some action you did or didn't take in response to what they thought was a request, address the issue of direct versus indirect communication. For example, "Since I missed what you were trying to tell me, it'd be great if you could say what's on your mind even if you think it's rude to be that direct."
- Observe and share. Over time, you may become conversant in their special language and be able to discern

a request in the midst of a lot of words and equivo-
cations. If you do, pass along what you've learned to
others who are mystified by this person!

<><><><><><><><><><><><><><><><><><><><><><><><><><><><><><><><><><><><><><><><><><><><><>

WORKSHEET:

IF YOU THINK YOU MAY BE A CIRCUITOUS TRAIN

Please answer the following questions with a yes or no. For
each yes answer, see the advice that follows the question.

**1. Do you find that others in your work group use a
more direct communication style and seem to consistently
misunderstand what you're trying to convey?**
You may need to make tweaks to align with the communication norms of your work group. What your family taught you,
or is typical of your culture, might be unreadable to others.

2. Do you make requests that go unanswered?
Ask for what you want using words that people understand.
Feeling resentful because no one has acted upon what you
thought you asked for is a clue you might need to adjust your
phrasing. Try out different words. Ask a trusted friend how
they would state a request.

**3. Are you afraid something bad will happen if you are more
direct in your communication?**
It's possible that your fears are overblown in your mind and
that the consequences aren't so dire. Is there any possibility
your anxiety keeps you from being clear with others? Or that
you like having justification for why you don't get what you
want? Consider practicing more assertive language (directly

117

asking for what you want) with a friend or loved one to get used to using this style of communication. You might find a happy medium between not-so-direct yet clear to the receiver.

<><><><><><><><><><><><><><><><><><><><><><><><><><><><><><><><><><><><><><><><><><><><><>

Summary for Dealing with Any Runaway-Train Jerk

- Remind yourself it's not personal. You won't take their behavior so personally if you realize they're an extreme version of what might be, in moderation, a valuable perspective. The exception is the Hazardous Materials Train, whose noxious gases are sickening at any level.
- Give feedback about how they're coming across if it makes sense to do so. It's quite possible they don't understand how significant their impact is on others.
- Sift through the cruddy packaging to see if there's a message that's worthy of attention. Is there something this person has to offer?
- Limit your exposure, or if it's really bad, get out. Extremes are hard to live with on a daily basis if there's no relief.

Chapter Six:

THE FIGHT-OR-FLEE JERK

This chapter is about conflict. Being a fighter or fleeing into the woodwork are two extremes of not handling conflict well. There will always be disagreements at work, and, in fact, it's a healthy way to expand thinking, creativity, and problem-solving. But there needs to be some path toward productive resolution. That's hard to achieve if people fight, flee, disengage, or try to bury it under the rug.

Most of the time, conflict at work is spawned by disagreements about roles (who is supposed to do what), goals (what the priority is), and how things get done (the processes or methods). However, we typically don't recognize this so conflict becomes personal and attributed to someone's personality. Then we make critical judgements about the person and retreat from a collegial relationship.

Values conflicts are more substantial because it's a disagreement about the "right" or "normal" way to see the world based on upbringing or culture. There are good references in the Additional Resources section for engaging in conversation regardless of the origin of the conflict. Since this is a book about work situations, I would encourage parties who have values conflicts to go back to basics you can agree upon: the underlying purpose and work of the organization that employs you.

An additional factor in how well we handle conflict is our personal tolerance for the raised voices that often come with disagreements or when someone is angry. I was a school social worker the first time a client yelled at me. A kid's parent was angry and shrieking over the phone. My heart rate sped up and my mouth went dry. I wanted to run! I put the receiver down on the desk and watched it carefully as the tirade continued. Finally, there was silence. I picked up the receiver and asked, "Are you mad at me?" The parent said no. That was my first lesson in "It's not always personal."

I had dreadful training at home about how to handle disagreements. My models were either violent arguments or notes slipped under the door in the dead of night. Really—notes! It's a no wonder I was ill-equipped to handle conflict on the job. My poorly developed skills meant I had to become informed about productive discord. Fortunately, I found useful books and knowledgeable coworkers.

You, too, may have had little, poor, or no training in how to handle conflict. You may be overly sensitive, frightened, or overly aggressive. Perhaps it's not you but a colleague who exhibits these traits. Or the culture of your organization has rules for airing discord that aren't healthy or productive.

This chapter won't delve into situations where people actually engage in fisticuffs, although I'm aware physical fights can occur at work. If that happens, my best advice is call security or law enforcement.

In this chapter, we'll cover:

- **The Chip-on-the-Shoulder the Size of an Elephant** (predisposed to fly off the handle)

- **The Smart-as-a-Whip and Hugely Defensive** (I know best, don't question me)
- **The Pot Stirrer** (setting others up to do battle)
- **The Disappearing Act** (flee!)
- **The Let's Make a Deal** (calm the waters—even when it's not needed)

The Chip-on-the-Shoulder the Size of an Elephant

We all have our sensitivities. Many of us can hide them until something touches a nerve, then we react like we've been stung by a hornet. For the person who has a huge chip on their shoulder, it takes very little to set them off. It's as if they have a neon sign blinking over their head saying, "I'm outraged!" and they come out swinging.

Other ways you might recognize this type:

- They can take an astonishing number of things personally. However, if you're around them long enough, you can predict what will send them over the edge.
- They have extreme emotional reactions to perceived injustices: crying, yelling, indignation, or fury.
- Their defensiveness is highly vocal, so you have to "duck and cover" if you hint at negative feedback.
- They may funnel most of their outrage onto one person who can't even blink right in their estimation.
- They have strong, indignant reactions that can prompt the team to either avoid them or be so careful that they exclude them from important discussions and decisions.
- They drive some people out of the group with their tantrums.

The Dramatic Director

It should be no surprise there can be a lot of off-stage drama between people who are trying to mount a production onstage. As a former amateur thespian, I had the privilege of working with a number of directors over the years. One had such a gigantic chip on her shoulder, it took next to nothing to knock it off—and bowl you over.

Natalie's bête noire was having anyone challenge her authority. She appeared to be a warm, welcoming presence on the surface and during the first reading. It took newbies by surprise when (by rehearsal three or four) a question or observation would set off a stream of pique. You wouldn't think that "Shouldn't I stand there instead?" or "I think this character is despondent, not angry," would require a dressing-down to put a performer in their place. Truly, you had to love acting to put up with someone skewering you just for proposing a costume idea that was different from Natalie's.

The obvious armchair-psychologist diagnosis was that Natalie was insecure. She didn't need to be because she really was a gifted director; she was smart, could exact fine performances from actors, and (at moments) was empathetic. On a good day, she was open to your ideas. She was lavish with praise at performances and cast parties. The positive mostly outweighed the negative, so people hung in. Inevitably, though, folks tired of the dynamics and moved on. But there was always a crop of willing fresh talent to take their places.

How to Deal with a Chip-on-the-Shoulder: Advice for Coworkers

- Understand that they believe they're justified. Arguing with them about how they feel doesn't work. Also realize that the definition of an overreaction is any reaction larger than your own.
- Know that the filter this person uses is based on some insecurity. It's pretty easy to figure it out because it's what they will accuse you of saying: "You think I'm (fill in the blank)." You may hear things like: not good

enough, stupid, unrealistic, pessimistic, too old, too young, unqualified, etc.

- Ask for their interpretation. If you receive an emotional response to something you said that wasn't intended to be provocative, you might ask, "What did you hear me say?" It's likely something went through their filter and came out garbled. Try again with, "Actually, that's not what I said," and repeat the message using different words. You may have to restate several times before it gets through.

- Intervene if it's helpful. If you're the bystander and have noticed a misinterpretation by the Chip-on-the-Shoulder, you may be able to intervene. If you can get the person to take a breath and calm down so they'll have a chance of listening, that's great. The fewer words the better to get their attention. For example, "Natalie, hang on and take a breath. I'm not sure you heard what David said." However, if their emotions are running high, they might not hear any clarification and start fighting with you as well.

- Choose how best to communicate your message. Verbal communication is tough, but written communication is worse for misinterpretation. If you think *anything* you have to say can be misinterpreted, use in-person communication (preferred) or virtual platform, or if you need to, phone. It's preferable to observe body language and hear tone of voice to correct misperceptions before they spin out of control.

- If it's a volunteer situation, like community theater, you may choose to pack up your talents and take them on the road to another group.

How to Deal with a Chip-on-the-Shoulder:
Advice for Managers

- Address disruptive behavior. If this person tanks every team meeting with their outbursts, try some of the suggestions from previous chapters on the Narcissist and the Know-It-All. In a private setting, the manager needs to be clear and direct about the offending behaviors and outline behaviors that are more acceptable.

- Examine your own words for anything that might prompt reactiveness in others. Are you inadvertently using language that is borderline accusatory? Is it demeaning, even if you didn't intend it to be? Try out your phrasing with a trusted ally who you know is good at building relationships. Statements like, "you should," "you must," "how could you," "why did you," "you always/never" are all blaming and should probably be banished from your repertoire.

- Address the issue in advance. It's important that you have a conversation about how you can give this person critical feedback in a manner that they can hear, understand, and act on. Do this *before* you need to give feedback. If they own up to having extreme reactions, ask how they want you to handle that.

- Provide guidance if they're open to it. If this person continues to be overly sensitive to team members' (or your) comments, you might suggest they seek help through coaching or counseling.

Worksheet:
If You Think You May Be a
Chip-on-the-Shoulder

Please answer the following questions with a yes or no. For each yes answer, see the advice that follows the question.

1. Are you aware of having a hair trigger for offense either because you're often offended or others have mentioned it?
You may be predisposed to the assumption that others are making demeaning comments about you. If so, that's a miserable way to live. You don't have to feel this bad, and your relationships can be a whole lot more fun. You might consider seeking counseling.

2. If you fly off the handle, do you ignore what people are trying to tell you about your interpretation?
If you get triggered by someone's comment, try turning down the siren in your head long enough to focus and really hear what they're saying. A calming breath or two will help.

3. Do you frequently find yourself taking offense?
That's another clue that your brain may not have translated their words accurately. Stop, breathe, and ask them to say it again. Let them know what you heard and ask if that's what they meant. It's possible they meant to be insulting, but probably not.

4. Do you continue to believe your intense reaction is justified?
Please understand that it's hard for others to be around you when you're in high drama mode.

The Smart-as-a-Whip and Hugely Defensive

There are people you want to rely on because of their expertise, but you're driven away after being exposed to their incredible defensiveness. They're at their best in lecture mode, providing facts and how to interpret them. Their recommendation sometimes comes in the form of an ultimatum. If you attempt to ask questions so you can understand their reasoning, it can send them into a prickly-cactus confrontation. And woe be it to you, decision maker, if the determination you make differs from their advice.

Other ways to recognize a Smart-as-a-Whip:

- They may have little patience for group process because in the past they've had their recommendations accepted without question or have been the sole decision maker.
- They may have reached a point in their career where they command a great deal of respect for their knowledge. As a result, they may consider it demeaning to be questioned.
- They may overwhelm you with facts and figures in an attempt to convince you of their "rightness" and get you to back off asking questions. This may be in the form of a verbal overload, or it may show up through over-the-top documentation.
- They may not be as expert as they want to be (e.g., new to the profession or just out of school), so they take any questioning as a slam to their knowledge. They're defensive in response because they're insecure.
- They think they're doing you a favor—which is true in a volunteer situation—so questioning their recommendations seems like a slap in the face. "I gave you my time and talent, and this is what I get in return?!"

Dee the Determined

Farouk came to me about one of his facilities planning directors, Dee. The executive team had asked the facilities planning department to evaluate one of the company's older structures. They wanted an assessment regarding whether to fix the building or tear it down and rebuild. Dee was lead on the evaluation, so Farouk brought her to the presentation. He wanted her to have a growth opportunity by speaking in front of the executives, and since it was her project, she had the required depth of knowledge.

Dee was no stranger to making presentations. She came to the meeting prepared with charts, estimated budgets, and a strong recommendation to tear down the structure and rebuild. It was the more expensive option, but there were good reasons to consider a new building that would be up to code and have flexibility for additional build-out space. Before Dee got into the detailed explanation of why this was her recommendation, one of the executives started asking questions about the assumptions Dee had used. The executive was trying to understand how the conclusion was drawn.

According to Farouk, Dee listened at first, then her posture stiffened, her jaw clenched, and her lips straightened into a thin line. Then she reached her limit. With a harsh tone, she castigated the executive, much to the embarrassment of Farouk. She didn't answer the question; she gave a "trust me, I know best" type of response. The executive tried again using conciliatory words. Her response continued to be defensive and she finished with, "Well, I guess it doesn't matter what I think." The executives sat in stunned silence while Farouk waited for the floor to open and swallow him. After a couple of seconds, he regained his composure and suggested they take a brief break. He headed for Dee.

Farouk told Dee that the questions weren't about her expertise; the executives needed to be brought up to speed.

They were the financially responsible parties for the organization, so it made sense they would want to understand the details, not just the conclusion. Bristling, Dee said she would have gotten to the details if she hadn't been interrupted. Farouk reminded her that it was *their* meeting, not hers, and they were welcome to interrupt at any time and go in the order that made sense to them. Dee calmed down enough to agree to answer questions but only if Farouk sat with her in front of the group to mediate if necessary. They got through the rest of the presentation.

Farouk told me that after that experience, he was reluctant to have Dee present to the executive team again. He said she had an attitude problem; I suggested it was a presentation preparation problem and wondered if Farouk would be willing to coach Dee. Since he saw her as an up-and-comer (if she could be less reactive), he was willing to invest time in her development. I suggested that the next time a high-stakes presentation was on the calendar, Farouk might arrange a practice run of Dee's talk. That way he, and other staff members, could drill her with likely questions. With some luck (and a reminder that questions weren't personal attacks) she might become less sensitive and be better equipped in the moment.

How to Deal with a Smart-as-a-Whip

- Use tentative language and take the burden of not understanding on yourself. For example, "You probably already said this, but I'm still a bit unclear about why you recommend silver instead of gold," or "I may have missed it, but could you remind us of the price of gold?"
- Bring up why you are asking questions if you notice the person is getting heated. For example, "I'm sure you're wondering why I'm asking a lot of questions rather than just saying yes to your recommendation.

It's because I have to thoroughly understand so I can accurately represent this to others," or "Dee, I don't want you to think that *you're* questionable; the questions are so *I* understand."

- Ask to be directed to the nugget you need for understanding. If their answer to a question leads to an overwhelming barrage of facts and figures, or voluminous documents in your email, ask them to identify the exact page(s) you should review.
- Find an alternate for high-stakes meetings. Unfortunately, the prickliness of the person can derail their contributions. If there's someone in the group who is less combative, you might consider asking them to make public appearances. They can take questions back to the expert to get answers.
- Be careful about how you use the expert. If you have your Smart-as-a-Whip sit on the side to answer specific questions at a presentation, it won't buy you much. The dynamic typically descends into contention once the questions start, regardless of who has been designated as the public face.

◇◇

WORKSHEET:

IF YOU THINK YOU MAY BE A SMART-AS-A-WHIP

Please answer the following questions with a yes or no. For each yes answer, see the advice that follows the question.

1. Do you hear questions as criticism?

That's not an unusual response. But if you know you're sensitive and tend to hear critique even when none is meant, that's about you. What is it you tell yourself? It's time to challenge that inner dialogue and switch to words that assume the best of the other person. Not this: "Why is she questioning me; can't she see I have much more knowledge than she does?" But this instead: "She can ask what she wants to know so I can tailor the information." Most of the time, questions aren't meant as a personal critique.

2. Even though you'll be in front of people or decision makers who are new to you, do you prepare a presentation as you always do?
Make sure you understand the goals of the meeting and why you're being asked to make a presentation. You might consider letting other people help you brainstorm the types of questions that could be asked. A person who knows the audience/personalities well, or who has experience with similar situations, can assist you in preparation.

3. Do you feel hyper before a presentation?
Use techniques that calm yourself so you have a better chance of remaining centered and able to respond. Things that can help are: exercise in the morning, visualization, meditation, a few deep breaths, and limiting your caffeine intake.

4. Are you sure you've understood the question?
You might want to gain clarity from the audience member before launching in. For example, "I want to make sure I'm answering your question. Is it to get information about the recommended vendor, or do you want to know why I'm recommending a vendor at all?"

The Pot Stirrer

When I was a teen, Aunt Rae warned me that Grandma Gladys was a master of stirring up family trouble. Grandma would carry a message like, "Grace got sick after eating your pumpkin pie," (true or not) to the pie maker just to incite them. Then she'd gleefully sit back while others duked it out.

I've noted similar dynamics in the workplace that started over unbelievably petty issues. The Pot Stirrer, when confronted, responds with statements like, "I'm just being honest," "Just sayin'," or "Don't shoot the messenger." This is an attempt to relieve the speaker of responsibility by implying, "It's not me; I'm just giving you the facts/passing this along—you should be thanking me!" I'd argue that the motivation behind delivering messages designed to enflame or hurt isn't benign.

You might recognize these attributes:

- They're good at setting up other people, but if *they're* gossiped about, they become victimized, hurt, or angry.
- They demonstrate a lack of empathy by passing along cruel comments.
- They collect and distribute stories; they delight in whispered conversations.
- They like the power derived from revealing information you don't have.
- They seek power/influence/status by trading information: "If I tell you this, what do you have for me?"

I'm-Just-Letting-You-Know Wanda

Song came to me about two of her staff members, Jodi (who had a knack for causing trouble) and Wanda, who had a compulsion to pass along information that was none of her business. This inevitably led to hurt feelings among coworkers.

Song reported that the latest blowup occurred the day before. Over the weekend, Jodi had taken her toddler son to swim lessons at the municipal pool and had run into Leesa, whose daughter was in the same class. On Monday morning, Jodi told Wanda that Leesa's daughter was more reluctant than the other kids to put her head in the water. For evidence, she showed a phone video of the kids in the pool. Jodi went on to speculate that the child was afraid because of Leesa's own anxiety about swimming.

Wanda went to Leesa assuming an air of sympathy about Leesa's daughter based on what Jodi had said. Leesa was well known for defending her youngster whenever the child was compared unfavorably to others. So it was no surprise that Leesa's response was anger at both Jodi and Wanda, to which Wanda retorted, "I saw the video and was trying to be nice!" Wanda reported back to Jodi that Leesa was mad about the video and supposition, so now all three were at odds and not speaking. The silence must've been welcome.

I'll admit that this type of tale sets my eyes rolling and I wonder, "Don't these people have enough to do?" Song assured me that everyone was aware of additional work begging to be done if they had an extra minute. I asked her if their group had an articulated set of norms (rules for how team members interact with each other). They didn't. I suggested she recruit a few staff volunteers who would be interested in working on this project with her. Song needed to be part of that group so she had the opportunity to assure something about gossip was included.

Song wondered about the legitimacy of addressing the swim class episode since it happened away from work and on the weekend. My counsel was that since the situation was brought into the workplace by Jodi and then Wanda got involved, Song needed to make it clear that gossiping about colleagues wasn't okay regardless of the venue.

When I checked back with Song, it appeared the anger-fest had dissipated among the three women after appropriate apologies had been extended and accepted. Against all odds, Jodi and Leesa were making swim playdates for their kids. When Song asked for volunteers from the staff to create departmental norms for communication, Wanda volunteered. Song hoped Wanda's participation would increase her ownership and compliance in upholding the norms. Wanda had vigorously affirmed her support of the no-gossip norm wording, although Song was on alert for any future Wanda-initiated storms.

How to Deal with the Pot Stirrer

- Don't approach this person to engage in gossip; that gives mixed messages about whether it's okay or not.
- Keep it to yourself. If someone reveals a personal story or one about someone else, *don't pass it along.*
- Refuse to engage. If someone approaches with gossip about you, you can always call them out with something like, "Why do you think I need to know this?" If the response is, "I thought you'd want to know what's being said about you," you can reply, "I don't. I'd appreciate it if you wouldn't pass along gossip." This applies to in-person approaches as well as email and text.
- Remove yourself. If you'd like to get out of the loop altogether, tell the person you aren't interested and that you have work to do. Then literally walk away from the conversation. This person (or group) will eventually stop coming to you since you're such a spoilsport.
- Switch it up with something positive. Please feel free to pass along praise to, and about, colleagues! This is a great way to combat the nastiness of departmental gossip. If you do it enough, it might catch on. For example, "Michael sure saved me today when I was overwhelmed with customers. I really appreciate how quickly he stepped up to help!" This can be

accomplished through virtual or in-person meetings, group email, or text threads.

<><><><><><><><><><><><><><><><><><><><><><><><><><><><><><><><><><><><>

WORKSHEET:

IF YOU THINK YOU MAY BE A POT STIRRER

Please answer the following questions with a yes or no. For each yes answer, see the advice that follows the question.

1. Do you believe it's up to you to pass along information that isn't yours?

I understand if you believe sharing good news is benign; however, good news or bad, the decision to reveal information resides with the person who owns the story. Honor their preferences for who knows and when they know. Unless you ask for (and receive) permission to relay their news, don't do it.

2. Do you think it's a passive act to set up a disagreement between others and then become a bystander?

Stop fooling yourself; it's not. That's an aggressive act. What do you get out of being hurtful? If it's to have power you feel you don't get in other ways, satisfy your need in a positive way, such as volunteering to organize something that needs to be done. If you set up conflict between others out of revenge because you believe one or more of the parties have harmed you, then I would suggest it's time to be more direct about your grievance so there's a possibility of resolving it.

3. Do you have trouble staying busy at work?

Find more tasks or help others out. It's not okay to cause discord as entertainment because you're bored. You're essentially stealing by wasting time that the company is paying for, plus you're tanking relationships.

4. Do you use speculation and gossip as a way to bond with colleagues?

Please find other things you have in common to discuss. There are literally millions of topics to talk about that have nothing to do with your coworkers' lives.

5. Are you aware of your motives for starting battles between people?

Regardless of the motive, it's important that you *stop* passing along confidences, your critical opinions about someone, or what other people are saying about a colleague or the boss. If anyone in your group is the subject of gossip, no one is safe—and that includes you.

◇◇

The Disappearing Act

In direct contrast to those who leap into conflict, some people flee the scene as if they hear a ticking bomb. Those who physically remove themselves when there's a whiff of disagreement are the most obvious. Others vacate mentally; they may have a deer-in-headlights look or slow to a crawl.

What you might notice about Disappearing Acts:

- They may have multiple triggers. Crises, busyness, and chaos can also have them running in the other direction.
- They may be highly anxious people.
- They may be lacking confidence in their judgment or knowledge.
- They may need order and predictability.

- Disagreement (especially when highly emotional) may be more than they can stand.

Warren the Dodger

Abel referred his newest promotion, Warren, to me. As Abel put it, Warren needed to increase his self-assurance in handling staff conflicts. Warren owned up to his discomfort with his workers' disagreements and said he felt he shouldn't have to be in the middle of sniping. His solution was to give them the opportunity to sort it out on their own. I asked how well that strategy was working; it wasn't.

Recently, a couple of staff members had gone around Warren to Abel when they needed help. Part of a manager's job is to mediate conflict or make a decision if one is needed. Abel made it clear he wasn't going to be Warren's "shadow manager," so this was a skill that Warren needed to develop.

When I met with Warren, I asked how he reacted to raised voices. He said he got a knot in his stomach and wanted to leave. I assured him that a lot of people felt that way, but he could learn to deal with it. Because conflict typically arrives with heated emotions, it can feel out of control and intimidating. However, it offers an opportunity to problem solve. Maybe if he kept his eye on the issue rather than the emotions, it would work better for him. I asked him to take note of his internal responses when anxiety-producing situations occurred over the next week.

When Warren returned, he reported two events had caused the familiar feeling of dread. I asked if he could identify the chatter in his head; it was "RUN!" I told him that the knot in his stomach and the imperative to flee were now his cues to consciously breathe and say positive things to himself, like, "You're okay; pay attention to the words."

Warren agreed to try the following when the next staff conflict arose:

- Keep his feet planted, take a good breath, and repeat the "you're okay" phrase to himself.
- Listen carefully so he could focus on the problem and avoid getting wrapped up in the emotion.
- Ask people to slow down if there was too much to absorb and/or lower their voices if they were yelling.
- Restate the issue to make sure he got it or have them further explain until he did understand.
- Ask the staff members to generate alternatives to see if they could resolve it themselves. If not, he could state his preference.
- Defer if he needed time to think.

The caveat to the last point was that he couldn't use deferral as a sophisticated way to escape. He'd need to tell the staff when they could expect a decision (the next day at the latest unless research was required). The best option was to engage his staff members in creating solutions thereby reinforcing they were capable of working out issues on their own.

The next week, Warren was successful in handling one situation and that gave him hope. He'd felt his stomach drop, but he didn't leave the room and the parties were able to reach an agreement. The second situation happened when Warren was on his way to a meeting. It was a conflict between two coworkers—he let it go and walked on. I suggested that in the future he could briefly intervene to acknowledge the disagreement and to let them know when he'd be back if they needed help to resolve it. Leaving with no comment made it appear that he was trying to ignore or escape.

Warren's skills continued to develop over time and he enjoyed more successes. One day I lingered to eavesdrop when I saw him speaking with three upset staff members. Warren summarized the issue and asked what they thought was the best course of action. They proposed differing solutions. He asked if they wanted to work it out or have him make the decision. They chose the latter. Warren stated his preference; would they be willing to do that? They agreed and went back to work.

I walked over to Warren to congratulate him on his skillful mediation and asked how that felt. He looked startled by the question and said he felt fine—clearly this had become second nature to him. Bravo!

How to Deal with the Disappearing Act: Advice for Coworkers

- Let them know their presence is needed. It's hard to work with someone who's physically or mentally absent. If your Disappearing Act shoves off when it's stressful (conflict, crisis, or high volumes), you can tell them (or your boss) that their participation is missed. What prevents them from helping out? You may find out they're lacking confidence and need more training or practice. Or that, like Warren, they're anxious in the face of discord.
- Don't settle for silence as an answer. If you rely on this person and they aren't responding to emails, calls, or texts, you may have to reach out multiple times to get communication going, or go to them in person (if that is an option). Don't give up because you think they should answer and you shouldn't have to keep asking. Go ahead and track them down. If you can't get an answer within a reasonable time frame, perhaps it's time to enlist your manager's assistance.
- Go out of your way to ask the opinion of your Disappearing Act. It may be that they feel they've nothing to offer or that no one would listen anyway. Give them a boost by acknowledging their good ideas and encourage them to contribute more often.

How to Deal with the Disappearing Act: Advice for Managers

- See the Disappearing Act's escape for yourself. If haven't witnessed their badly timed departure yourself, you may need to drop by often enough to see what's really happening. It's a lot easier to give feedback about something you've directly observed than to base it on third-party reports. Then reinforce your expectations for their involvement but be sure to ask for their concerns so you can address them.
- Ask questions and listen. Does this person need more specific training or coaching to feel more confident in their work or in addressing disagreements? Your human resources department may provide offerings.

‹‹‹

WORKSHEET:

IF YOU THINK YOU MAY BE A DISAPPEARING ACT

Please answer the following questions with a yes or no. For each yes answer, see the advice that follows the question.

1. Do you have anxiety that prevents you from being part of discussions if they are heated or there's obvious disagreement?

Dealing with conflict is part of any job. Healthy disagreement leads to improvements in work process, so your voice needs to be heard. You might want to speak with your physician or a counselor for help if your emotional reaction is preventing your ability to stay engaged during disagreements or conflict situations.

2. Do you have intense reactions to conflict? Can you identify your physical reactions to conflict as well as what you say to yourself?

These reactions are your cues to say something reassuring to yourself and talk yourself down. Words like, "You're okay, you're not in danger," or "Take a breath, you're fine," or "You can figure this out." Again, counseling may be of help.

3. Do you lose your train of thought when you're anxious?

Let the person know that disagreement is hard for you and ask them to repeat what they said. If anxiety has caused you to lose track of the conversation, pay close attention to their words. Really listen to understand (which means lowering your own reaction). If you find yourself reacting strongly to an email or text, take a moment to calm, then reread it. As a result of anxiety, your brain may have inserted meaning that wasn't intended.

4. Do you feel like you're floating out of your body when there's conflict?

Tell yourself to feel your feet or fingers if you find yourself so preoccupied with your thoughts that you are unable to hear what's being said. That'll get you back into your body and in the moment, rather than paying attention to panicky voices in your head.

5. Do you assume that every conflict between colleagues should go up the chain of command?

Most managers expect coworkers to attempt to resolve disagreements before elevating concerns to management. If you aren't sure what the expectations are, ask your boss.

6. Do you flee as soon as conflict appears?

Choose an issue that's not too threatening or one in which

you aren't terribly invested so you can build your tolerance. Over time, you might be able to build your resilience to stay engaged when situations are more intense.

7. Are there any resources available at work to learn about conflict strategies?

Consider attending classes on how to handle conflict if they're offered. Community colleges may have classes, or you could look online. There are great books as well; see the Additional Resources section.

8. Is your voice unheard because you can't step up to disagreement?

In that case, you need to realize decisions will be made without you. And at that point, you've lost your right to complain. Hopefully that's enough incentive to encourage you to speak up.

9. Are you the manager?

Handling conflict is an essential skill for your position. If you regularly walk away from discord among your staff members or with your peers, it's probably noticed—negatively. It's important you develop conflict resolution skills through training and/or coaching.

<><><><><><><><><><><><><><><><><><><><><><><><><><><><><><><><><><><><>

The Let's Make a Deal

We count on peacemakers because they possess the ability to untangle communication and cut through differences. They're diplomats and negotiators who possess the invaluable skill of being able to identify common interests. They don't stifle dissension; they provide a platform for the full disclosure of concerns and the maintenance of civility.

In contrast, there are people who are so uncomfortable with conflict that they sweep it under the rug or quickly broker a deal to end *their* discomfort. Although they may be hoping to squelch strong emotions, that rarely works. The conflict simmers along under the surface and does even more damage. Sometimes you need to fully air differences before you can come to a productive solution. Their entreaty to "get along" under any and all circumstances undermines that.

For some people it's habit rather than discomfort that drives them to quell disagreement. A frequently used strategy is compromise (give and take), which is a viable option when time is limited. What may be used on a daily basis to resolve modest concerns can be far less effective for important decisions. Taking the time for a lengthier and more thoughtful exploration of the issues could lead to a better and more durable outcome through consensus.

What you might notice about those who quickly want to stop dissenting voices:

- They may be overly solicitous to get everyone to "be nice" and end disagreement.
- They may get panicky when they hear excited voices even if you think you're having a lively discussion and there's no conflict.
- Their need for amiability may cause them to intervene when it's not necessary, which comes across as intrusive and patronizing.
- They may rush to compromise even when it's needless.
- They are so intent on finding a middle ground between others' opinions that you may never hear their ideas.

Jacob the Sweeper

As my conflict workshop ended, two of the participants approached me for help with their boss, Jacob. Marty and

142

Taylor asked how to handle a boss who was intolerant of even minor disagreements. Whenever he overheard coworkers in animated discussion, Jacob would trot over to calm the waters. His first comment was, "There's nothing so bad that we need to fight about it."

The staff felt Jacob's behavior was like a parent swooping in to break up fighting children, which they found unnecessary and demeaning. They provided me with an example. The two of them were working on software implementation and having an animated discussion about potential incompatibility issues. They had a difference of opinion about how to proceed. Taylor emphatically argued for more research because these issues are messy to clean up. Marty insisted that the vendor of this popular software had all problems well documented. Taylor had just started to suggest that they call a colleague at another company to ask about their experience when Jacob zoomed in to interrupt.

He started with his usual, "There's nothing so bad that we need to fight about it." As they started to tell Jacob about the issue, he interrupted to end what he thought was discord by proposing an inadequate solution. When Taylor and Marty both recommended calling a peer at a similar company, Jacob backed down. While that wasn't a bad alternative, what Jacob didn't realize was they would've said anything to get him to go away.

Marty and Taylor found Jacob's frequent intervention annoying and stifling. What disturbed them (and others on staff) was that they wanted to have healthy debates in meetings so they could hear *all* opinions. But if voices became animated, Jacob would end the discussion with compromises or spontaneous (and often mystifying) decisions.

Taylor and Marty wanted me to force their boss to attend the conflict class. If people had been able to nominate their bosses to attend training, I never would've had an empty seat. Instead, I asked if one of them would be comfortable approaching Jacob. Taylor volunteered. I suggested she say that in her opinion the team was seasoned enough to handle a debate-style approach to problem-solving. If people could freely discuss the pros and cons of various solutions, they were more likely to come to consensus where all parties agreed to support a direction, at least on a trial basis. Since the entire staff had to implement these decisions, it made good sense that they all have ownership. What did Jacob think?

If Jacob thought it was a good idea, then they could discuss format. If Jacob thought that was too risky, Taylor could offer to have him observe one of her meetings with Marty where they used this approach.

I heard back from Taylor that Jacob agreed to the more conservative option. Jacob observed a meeting and was impressed, even though he wasn't used to the high-spirited discussion. The outcome reached was solid, so Jacob said he might try using a debate-style discussion at a staff meeting. Taylor and Marty quickly volunteered to facilitate.

How to Deal with a Let's Make a Deal

- Consider the possibility that a low tolerance for disagreement is the problem. If your Let's Make a Deal person attempts to stop the flow of conversation because raised voices upset them, it's likely they have trouble with conflict. If they interrupt a worthwhile discussion, you might try saying something like, "We're not fighting and would like to continue; it's okay if you want to step away."
- Appeal to their desire for a permanent resolution. If this person wants a quick decision and cuts off problem-solving prematurely, engage them by saying something like, "If we spend a couple of more minutes on this now, we won't need to revisit it later."
- Use a variety of methods to get through. If yours is a boss who has a low threshold for differing opinions and

144

quickly intrudes to end what they consider to be disputes, your team may have better luck expressing themselves in one-on-one conversations (although it would be helpful if the team members were all on the same page). Alternatively, you can write your opinions in email with an ask to discuss it later. This gives them the benefit of time to reflect and calm down before responding.

- Consider recruiting a facilitator. If your team really needs to air a controversial subject and your boss is reluctant to be the moderator (or refuses to entertain the topic at all), you might suggest seeking a facilitator from human resources or asking another manager to moderate.

- Determine the best strategy. If your team compromises so quickly they end up with watered-down solutions because of too many trade-offs, it's okay to question whether it's the best decision-making option for the situation. Perhaps an individual's choice would work, or consensus (i.e., we all agree to support a decision), or a vote.

<hr>

WORKSHEET:

IF YOU THINK YOU MAY BE A LET'S MAKE A DEAL

Please answer the following questions with a yes or no. For each yes answer, see the advice that follows the question.

1. Are you driven to end any whiff of conflict?

There's a difference between intervening to maintain civility and abruptly calling a halt to a disagreement due to *your* anxiety. If your actions are driven by fear, you can use the stress tools noted in the Disappearing Act section of this chapter. Specifically, identify the cues that prompt you to leap into action and become aware of what you say to yourself about the situation. If you can become more aware of moving into your "red zone," you'll know when it's time to talk yourself down. The goal is to be able to make decisions or act based on reason, not impulse, when you're feeling uncomfortable.

2. Do you intervene to "smooth the waters" when people are trying to work things out?

Give situations an opportunity to resolve on their own. If you interrupt, you throw others off their stride before they've had a chance to express themselves. However, feel free to intervene to maintain civility if people are attacking each other by name-calling or blaming.

3. Did you grow up in a family where it wasn't okay for people to be animated or express disapproval?

You may need to learn how to "let it be" and not run to the rescue. This requires you to notice your desire to jump in. Instead, breathe, relax the tension in your body, and tell yourself you're safe; there's no need to act.

4. Has your experience taught you that all conflict results in irreparably damaged relationships?

When ties are severed, it's most likely because the argument became personal in nature. Many conflicts at work are based on three issues: roles (who's supposed to do what), goals (what's the priority), and how to get the job done (methods or processes). See if you can identify the underlying source of conflict so you don't see it as personal.

5. Do you know people who disagree yet enjoy a good relationship?

Observe how they interact when they have a disagreement as well as after they've come to agreement or have agreed to disagree. There's something to be learned from them.

6. Are you unaware of other options besides compromise to end a conflict?

Compromise is one option, but it may not be the best when you need a durable solution, or a more expedient one. You can increase your conflict resolution tools through classes, coaching, counseling, or reading (see Additional Resources). It takes practice to become proficient, so don't get discouraged.

◇◇◇

Summary How to Deal with Any Fight-or-Flee Jerk

- Be prepared. With the more aggressive fighters, giving feedback is likely to get you a defensive response in return. Don't be scared, just prepare for their bark. They might modify their behavior anyway, so keep an eye out.
- Engage in positive conversations to build collegial relationships. Some people bond with colleagues by gossiping. When you're new, it feels good to be accepted and have people confide in you about other coworkers. You may not realize how destructive participating in a gossip culture can be, so avoid it.
- Just say no to gossip. You can give gentle feedback by saying something like, "I'm sure it's not your intention, but when you pass along stories about coworkers, people tend to get upset."
- Know thyself. Some of us are wired up to be more volatile (remember Evan, the manager in the Incompetent Jerk chapter?). If this is a cultural or family norm, you may need to turn down the volume at work. People do

differ, and there's a range of acceptable behaviors; it's the extreme that needs to be reined in.

- Be a good role model. People who want to flee or need to rapidly resolve disagreements may require reassurance that discord can lead to productive results. If they only see damaged relationships, it further promotes their habitual responses. Make sure you demonstrate productive conflict strategies yourself.

- Consider training or coaching. Not that many people grew up with positive examples for handling conflict. You and your team might benefit from instruction or coaching on how to disagree and achieve positive outcomes. Speak with your human resources department about classes and meeting facilitators.

- Clarify and abide by group norms. Group norms can help everyone understand the rules of the road for disagreement, communication, and other important issues related to working together. If you're the manager, be sure to discuss these. If you're a staff member and the norms aren't clear, please ask your manager to address them with the entire team.

Chapter Seven:

THE POOR ME JERK

This chapter is about people who feel helpless or at the mercy of others. A victim mentality isn't dictated by actual conditions. Some people see their situation as being hostile and dangerous even when others in the same position don't. There are those who appear to have it made yet suffer from paralyzing fear or a belief that they have no agency over their life.

How much is belief and how much is circumstance? Some people *do* live in a limited or dangerous world. Their attitude doesn't change the facts, but it can change their experience.

At work there's no simple calculus to identify what's in our control and what's not. Colleagues who feel (or are) powerless or frightened provide challenges for their coworkers. We also know discrimination isn't just a belief—it exists and is demonstrated, individually and institutionally. Those who claim to be marginalized may very well have valid complaints.

In this chapter we'll explore the following experiences of helplessness at work:

- **The Quaking-in-Their-Boots** (I'm afraid!)
- **The Why Me?** (things never go well for me . . .)
- **The Take Care of Me** (help me out, again)
- **The Complainers** (and here's another thing wrong)

The Quaking-in-Their-Boots

Coworkers who are inordinately fearful can be troublesome because they tend to be passive and terrified of drawing attention. Imagine how hard it was for them to interview for the job. They may have a lot to offer, but you'd never know it because they intentionally fade into the background.

They may be identified by some of the following characteristics:

- They find coping mechanisms to avoid the part of the job that's scary. For example, they may routinely request others do the feared task, saying they're not good at it.
- Their level of anxiety can run from the extreme of becoming paralyzed when faced with their fear to actually doing the work but making excuses for a poor level of quality.
- They may discount how important this skill is to their work. For example, "Speaking up in meetings isn't critical to my job."
- They may channel their worry into a frenzy of preparation that ends up sabotaging their ability to perform well. For example, staying up all night to prepare a presentation, diving into incomprehensible detail, or spending an inordinate amount of time on the visuals without practicing the actual talk.
- They may attempt to do the feared task, for example cold-calling, which (in their nervousness) they execute poorly, thereby reinforcing their belief that they're incapable and deservedly afraid.

- They may be willing to live with the negative consequences to their career rather than tackling the problem.

Choked Chayla

Jamal asked if I would be willing to coach his employee, Chayla. He said she was so timid that if he called on her in a staff meeting, she left the room. Chayla was highly skilled and had developed written protocols that needed to be presented to various groups starting with her own. He knew that if he insisted she address her coworkers, she'd probably quit. Jamal asked if I might help Chayla with her fear of public speaking. His eventual goal was for her to provide project updates at team meetings. I warned Jamal that Chayla needed to be willing to engage in this work. If she was, we'd be taking baby steps; this wasn't going to be a quick fix.

Chayla showed up to my office at the appointed time, but she didn't knock on the door. She stood in the hallway like she was waiting to be called into the principal's office. I felt like a trumpeting elephant in the face of her nervousness and barely audible voice. Her hand shook and she frequently dropped her eyes to the table.

When I asked Chayla what she wanted from our time together, she had no answer. She'd been sent by her boss and didn't want to disappoint him or get in trouble. She knew Jamal wanted her to make presentations, and she was petrified. With tears in her eyes, she asked me to relay to him that she couldn't do it and that he was asking too much. Just the thought of having to speak in public made her forehead and upper lip bead up with sweat.

I switched gears and asked about her career dreams. She said she wanted to head up a program but not manage people. Given Jamal's assessment of her work quality, that sounded like a distinct possibility. But she'd need to represent her program to others—she knew that, right? She nodded. I asked if she was willing to break through that barrier now or continue to hope that it'd get better on its own. She really wanted to believe this issue would resolve itself but knew it wouldn't. Her desire to move ahead in her career was in competition with her fears. Privately, I was concerned that Chayla's anxiety was beyond the scope of our work together and wondered if I should suggest she see her physician for additional help.

Fortunately, when Chayla came back and we were focused on her area of expertise, she became calmer and more self-assured. She brought me a few talking points about the protocols she'd written. Together we developed a script for a two-minute presentation. She read it to me a few times, then created a bullet point outline to decrease her reliance on notes. I asked her to practice giving the talk to someone at home.

Chayla continued to work on expanding her presentation and practicing it. Within a couple of months, she gave a ten-minute speech to Jamal and, finally, to her team. She received lavish praise each time, which boosted her confidence immeasurably.

Eventually, Chayla registered for the company's public speaking class to further chip away at her fear. Both Chayla and Jamal were happy with her progress and felt she was ready to consider applying for program manager openings.

How to Deal with a Quaking-in-Their-Boots: Advice for Coworkers

- Bring it out in the open. Colleagues are often the first to notice a coworker's lack of ability (or unwillingness) to do a task because *they* end up picking up the slack. If you're the burdened colleague, ask if your reluctant teammate needs additional training. If you can provide it, fine, but you can always refer them back to your manager for help. If they still refuse to do this duty, let them know you won't be able to continue to do their work for them. Speak with your manager if the situation persists.

How to Deal with a Quaking-in-Their-Boots: Advice for Managers

- Ask the person what's preventing them from doing the assignment. If it's a required skill, then be clear about performance expectations. Provide the help they need to gain mastery. If it's something that isn't mandatory, perhaps you can assign duties that play to their strengths. But beware of unfairly distributing work to those who already have a job to do.

- Identify your role in the problem. If you hired without being clear about job requirements that included this particular function, it was your oversight. You owe it to the employee to try to find a mutually acceptable solution.

- Suggest additional help. You might recommend your Quaking-in-Their-Boots seek additional assistance from a health-care provider or counselor.

- Question your own motives if you have career plans for someone that they don't have for themselves. It's great to encourage growth but, in the end, it's *their* life and career.

<<<><><><><><><><><><><><><><><><><><><><><><><><><><><><><><><><><><><><><><>

WORKSHEET:
IF YOU THINK YOU MAY BE A
QUAKING-IN-THEIR-BOOTS

Please answer the following questions with a yes or no. For each yes answer, see the advice that follows the question.

1. Are you scared about doing some part of your job?
Clarify what is frightening and why. Then it's time to risk talking with your manager. Pretending, lying, or deflecting are ill-fated long-term strategies. Expecting your colleagues to pick up your share is an unfair burden to them. Perhaps training or practice can help you master this challenge.

2. Did you say you could do something that you knew you couldn't (or hoped you could but now realize you can't)?
If so, you'll need to negotiate with your supervisor. If this is a critical part of the job, you may need to find another position.

3. Was this critical task not revealed initially through the job description or interview?
If you know you wouldn't have accepted the position if had it been, your boss has some responsibility to help resolve this. The category of "other duties as assigned" should be reserved for lesser job functions or the inevitable changes that occur over time, not a major task for which you were ill-equipped or unprepared.

4. Have the position requirements changed sufficiently over time that they now include duties you don't know how to perform?

If so, ask for training. There are additional ideas in the Left-to-Languish section in the chapter on Incompetent Jerks.

5. Are you limiting your career choices out of fear (public speaking, for example)?
Please understand that there's plenty of help out there—including medication, if appropriate. I hope you'll seek assistance through coaching, counseling, classes, support groups, or online videos. You owe it to yourself to be unfettered by anxiety that limits your work options.

‹‹

The Why Me?
The Why Me always seems to be whining: I never move up, I'm ignored, I can't get a break, etc. People who feel helpless in this way assume everyone else has it better. They see the world as a zero-sum game: anyone with more money/skill/talent/knowledge/education has lessened the Why Me's opportunities. They're envious and bitterly jealous. This pervasive belief most likely started early in life, and it's a hard one to shake. There's both a finality to this state ("This is the way it is,") and a passiveness ("As a result, I can't do anything about it."). All of us can go through rough patches when life feels unfair. The Why Me's victimized state isn't transitory; it's a persona that endures.

You'll recognize them by some of the following:

- They point fingers at "them" as the cause of their suffering.
- They may not believe in themselves enough to seek education, training, certification, or mentoring to move up.
- They play out their pattern with next-to-no insight that they're the common denominator in every situation.

- They have little interest in self-awareness. After a particularly ego-damaging event, they may ask the question, "Why does this happen?" but the window of vulnerability is brief before they're back to blaming others.
- They may be desperate to feel special and attempt to damage others' reputations to gain sought-after status. They may use criticism, gossip, or lies to make someone else "less" so they can be "more."
- They may spew vitriol about work, local, national, or world conditions—as if that, in itself, is a contribution to solving them.

Wailing Wendy

A number of years ago, an acquaintance introduced me to Wendy whom I saw with some regularity. I admired Wendy's intellect and humor, but her frequent claim of victim status was tiresome. She had a lot going for her, but rather than count her blessings, she engaged in a lot of complaining; nothing was ever good enough. Money was the pet focus, and she was constantly on the edge of financial ruin. Eventually, her fear became so overwhelming that she shut down her business and found a job.

Prior to opening her consultancy, Wendy had left full-time employment due to a terrible boss. You won't be surprised to learn that no matter where she was, Wendy had a crappy supervisor. The next job was no different. She'd previously known this woman as a colleague and thought she was terrific. However, within weeks of her new gig, the old laments began: I don't get enough recognition, other people get more acknowledgment than I do, no one talks to me, I'm treated differently than everyone else, I don't know how I'm doing because the boss won't tell me, I'm not paid enough, other people receive more. You get the picture.

Thanks to her insecurities, she was a pain in the patootie. No amount of praise was enough; she needed to be the favorite. She wanted people to include her but did nothing to make herself someone others would want to befriend. She wore her neediness like a coat of flypaper. No wonder colleagues steered clear of her.

Eventually, Wendy's mounting anxiety led to her most feared conclusion: she was fired. She'd become a temperamental leech to her boss and too difficult for coworkers to handle. Although she'd repeatedly played out this scenario in her career, she continued to lack any insight about her contributions.

It's hard to be friends with someone like this—at work, or anywhere for that matter. It isn't a mutual relationship: one side always needs (or demands) more.

How to Deal with a Why Me: Advice for Coworkers

Recognize that you are up against someone's basic beliefs about themselves and the world. Beliefs are the rules we've set for how life works, so it's hard (but not impossible) to challenge them. You're unlikely to change anyone's mind, but you might be able to help them reconsider their thinking.

Here are some ideas:

- State the belief. It's possible they've had this background noise running through their head for so long they're not even aware of it. Here's an example of a belief you might call out based on what you've heard them say: "Sounds like you think it's not worth completing an education at your age." They might be surprised to hear that's what they believe.
- Counter with contrary evidence. "Liz just got her degree and she's older than you." You'll probably get a "yes, but" earful about why Liz is special, but it's worth a try.
- Ask a question like, "Why do you think that's true?" This pushes them to explain the rationale behind the

157

belief. Of course, *you* don't need to understand, but *they* do. Sometimes what they say is so nonsensical they'll stop to reconsider.

- Decide how willing you are to invest in this person. How much you're drained (or not) by them has to do with the amount of energy you've got available.
- Try establishing parameters for your interactions. For example, you can set up a time limit for how long you'll listen to their litany of work problems. You can say something like, "Wendy, you've got five more minutes to talk about how awful your boss is. The timer is on—go!" Don't be surprised if you have to revisit these "rules" every so often (or frequently!).

How to Deal with a Why Me: Advice for Managers

- Review the guidance above for coworkers to see what might apply in your situation.
- Set up guidelines about how much you can, or will, attend to their needs. Even if you could provide constant praise or reassurance, it'll never be enough to offset their insecurity.
- Help them recognize the indicators of when they've done a good job so they can give themselves a pat on the back and not need so much from you.

×××

WORKSHEET:

IF YOU THINK YOU MAY BE A WHY ME

Please answer the following questions with a yes or no. For each yes answer, see the advice that follows the question.

1. Do you feel you always get the rotten end of the stick?

It is possible life is always unfair to you, but it could also be a pretty normal balance between things going well and not so well. If you've envied other people and focused solely on their victories, you likely missed the challenges that also came their way.

2. Has whining or blaming others become a large part of your conversational repertoire?

You need to know that it's tedious for others. Expand your conversational horizons by talking about books, movies, food, current events, anything but how bad things are for you.

3. Do you sabotage coworkers to make yourself feel better or to appear more skilled/talented/competent than they are?

Not only do people see through this, it's a career limiting move for you. If your self-esteem is in that much trouble, I would highly recommend you seek counseling.

4. Is there always a colleague who is the cause of your suffering?

Ask yourself the uncomfortable question, "What's my contribution?" You're the constant factor in each of these situations. Most people get along with colleagues, at least superficially, most of the time.

5. Are you aware that you complain a lot?

This can very well limit your career opportunities. If it's a habit, I'd invite you to break it. See the advice following question 2 and find other things to talk about. It takes time to change habits, so keep at it.

6. Do you shut down feedback that implies you might be the problem?

You may have even requested feedback in the aftermath of a particularly traumatic event, but did you really want it or were you asking for confirmation that what you did was fine? Arguing with or punishing those who attempt to provide insight into your behavior will silence them, and they're unlikely to be honest with you in the future. If someone cares enough to alert you to actions that limit you, be gracious enough to listen without argument.

7. Is your pattern to blame others and see yourself as victimized?

I hope you'll consider seeking counseling to assist you in exploring these issues so you can open to other perspectives.

‹‹›››

The Take Care of Me

There are some people who expect to be taken care of by others and trust this will happen—because it always has. I sometimes wonder if they were the youngest child where the constant refrain to siblings was, "Watch out for the baby!" Somehow, the natural consequences that befall the rest of us as a result of flaky behavior don't happen to them. Nor are they aware of their good fortune because this is how things are. As Blanche DuBois said in Tennessee Williams' *A Streetcar Named Desire*, "I have always relied on the kindness of strangers."

At work, this is the colleague who frequently asks for help (hopefully with an ingratiating smile). We *all* need help at various times. The difference is their requests are habitual, and it's presumed you'll pitch in. They don't remember how to do things that they should've mastered by now. It's easier to ask you than to figure it out or look it up. They may have a winsome lost puppy look that draws you in or be so doggone friendly and appreciative that you find yourself saving them over and over. At some point you may come to the end of your rope and want them to finally learn how to put paper in the copy machine or tally the numbers they're paid to compile.

They may be recognized by one or more of the following characteristics:

- They may be completely unaware their repeated requests are a burden, especially if this is a lifelong pattern and people have always rescued them.
- They collapse into tears or helplessness, expecting to be saved. There's a degree of manipulation going on. This version of the Take Care of Me isn't as winsome as the more charming ones.
- They may have learning issues. Perhaps they've never been taught in a manner they can retain.
- They may be in the wrong job.
- They may have other wonderful and needed skills, so the missing ones aren't that big a deal (unless you're the one fulfilling them).

Comfortable Christopher

Cadence came to talk to me after a class on dealing with difficult people. Her problem wasn't that her coworker Christopher had a problematic personality; it was that she regularly found herself doing the written part of his job. Most of the time it was okay because she liked to write, but there were times when she didn't appreciate the added burden. Christopher just assumed that she'd do it.

Cadence wondered if she could change the "rules" with him now that the pattern had been so well established. I asked her what she wanted. She hoped to have Christopher pick up some part of the duties that had fallen to her. Did she think she could talk with him about that? She did. Sometimes gaining clarity about what you want can make all the difference.

I got an email from Cadence that she'd spoken with Christopher and he was fine doing more of the research in trade for her doing the writing; it played to their individual strengths. He apologized for not realizing he'd been imposing on her.

How to Deal with a Take Care of Me

- Make an exchange if possible. If you're asked to do the same thing for them frequently, is there a trade that could be made like the one between Cadence and Christopher?
- Have them rely on prompts. If this is a task they don't do often, make sure they create learning aids so they can remember how to do it on their own in the future.
- Praise them when they do it on their own. Some people are stingy with compliments because they think, "It's about time they did it!" We tend to repeat actions for which we've been given positive notice. Want them to continue? Use praise. Even something simple like, "You did it!" works (but only if the voice tone is sincere!).
- Notice your role in their helplessness. If they're slow or poor at completing the task, do you take over because *you* can't stand it? If so, you're complicit. You can teach them and stop doing it or do it graciously.
- Show them what quality looks like so they can produce at a higher level. Think of a household member who doesn't clean to your standards. Point out what "clean" looks like to you. But if someone's engaged

in vacuuming or washing the dishes and you continue to grumble and then take it out of their hands to do yourself, you're shooting yourself in the foot.

<>>>

WORKSHEET:

IF YOU THINK YOU MAY BE A TAKE CARE OF ME

Please answer the following questions with a yes or no. For each yes answer, see the advice that follows the question.

1. Do you recognize yourself from the description?
If so, then you're aware that you're frequently asking others to do parts of your job. Did you take employment for which you're unqualified? Are you unwilling to put in the effort to learn? If you want to keep this position, ask your boss for more training and apply yourself to mastering the needed skills.

2. Are you hoping you can get someone else to do the parts of your job that you don't like?
Well, who wouldn't want that luxury! But it's inequitable. The rest of your team is doing the job, so you can too.

3. Even if you aren't doing the entirety of the job, do you have skills that are so extraordinary and you perform them so splendidly that your manager is willing to turn a blind eye to what you *aren't* doing?
If that's the case, ask that your job description be updated to reflect reality. Your new position should be explained to your peers, as they've no doubt noticed you've had a pass on the duties they still have to fulfill.

<>>>

The Complainers—Are They Justified?

I swear there are some people who face the new day with a petulant voice and a "Is it sunny *again*?" attitude. Even the most benign comment from them sounds whiny. It's the tone of voice, the choice of words, and a defensive posture. When the habitual packaging of their message is so unappealing, it's easy to tune them out, fight with them, or avoid them. Yet sometimes they have something important to say and we miss it.

It's also easy to ignore complaints that are inconvenient because the problem's too difficult to remediate, you don't have the authority or knowledge to do anything about it, it's too widespread, or it says something about you that you don't want to know or acknowledge, among many other excuses. Because it's unpalatable, we may not even recognize that a problem has been brought up. Or we hear it but want to ascribe a difficult personality to the person who had the courage to speak.

Here are some thoughts on legitimate complaints that may get short shrift:

- Saying that one can't get ahead because the deck is stacked against them. This may well be true. Discrimination exists for large classes of people as well as individuals. How unbiased are your company's hiring and promotional practices? Most orchestral symphonies engage in nondiscriminatory auditioning. They put the candidate musician behind a curtain or screen so the only evaluation the hiring committee can make is based on ability.
- Complaints they're always passed over for promotion. There could be a lack of communicated expectations and performance feedback. Unqualified people desire, and expect, promotions with no idea why they don't get them. When we don't know what "qualified" is

and feel we haven't been given a chance, we look to what's different about us (e.g., gender, race, ethnicity, age, etc.) as the reason for losing out. Managers need to be clear about the specific skills/tasks that must be mastered, and the level of experience required for promotion.

- Complaints about unreasonable work demands. Do we presume that those behind us should be made to suffer and pay the dues we did? It's one thing to expect that workers have enough experience to be competent in the role, it's another to expect them to walk on hot coals because you had to go through a similar hazing ritual. For example, if the only way a woman was able to get a leadership position meant putting in sixty-hour workweeks (thereby missing her kid's childhood), the expectation that her younger colleagues do the same is unreasonable. If it was wrong then, it's still wrong.

How to Deal with Complainers

- Ask yourself if they're right. It's healthy to question one's own biases and look at the prevailing culture of an organization. If they're pointing out illegal behavior or practices, then it needs to be reported to the appropriate authorities.
- Determine your approach. If it's a garden-variety complainer who has something negative to say about everything, look for help in the High-Speed Train Jerk chapter, How to Deal with a Funeral Train. Whiny? The section on Why Me in this chapter may help. Overly critiqued by a boss? Look at the section on How to Deal with the Meddlesome Manager in the Know-It-All Jerk chapter.
- Communicate qualifications clearly. If the person complaining about lack of career opportunity isn't qualified

to move up and no one has ever told them, it's a kindness to discuss requirements and how to obtain the training or experience to become a viable candidate.

- Take a chance on being (gently) honest. Along the same lines of stalled career growth (and grumbling about it), does an annoying personality keep them from advancement? Does their communication style keep people from hearing what they have to say? Again, it's kinder to share what you've noticed than to let them continue to blunder along thinking it's all out of their control. Say something like, "I have an observation about what might be getting in your way. Would you like to hear it?" You might get a no. Even if you get a yes, you may get a defensive reaction (as can happen with any feedback). It's possible they'll think about what you say and recognize their contribution to the problem.

- Be a mentor or advocate. If you have more power in the system than those who complain they can't get ahead, can you mentor or provide them with contacts who might help them? Can you advocate for changes brought up by those with a lesser voice?

Worksheet:

If You Think You May Be a Complainer

Please answer the following questions with a yes or no. For each yes answer, see the advice that follows the question.

1. Is your career stalled?

Even if it scares you, learn what's getting in your way. It may be technical skills, experience, communication skills, education, or training. Or perhaps it's something subtle, like how you address people and problems. Ask your boss for an honest evaluation of what it would take for you to move ahead. Or ask someone in the job you aspire to obtain what the qualifications are. Once you know, you have a path forward. Without information you risk being stuck for a very long time.

2. Do you believe you're being discriminated against?
If so, seek help from human resources, your union, the Equal Employment Opportunity Commission, or an employment lawyer in your area (make sure you understand how they charge for services).

3. Have you been getting little response to the issues you bring up the chain of command?
Coalitions sometimes work better than tackling a systemic issue on your own. See if there are allies you could join to approach those with more power to relay your collective point of view.

4. Do you only bring complaints?
Showing up with ideas of what would work can be more helpful than doing a hit-and-run dump of a problem. For example, if you believe you or others have been excluded from promotional opportunities, you could propose that managers take a class on how to develop their people. Or ask that performance appraisals evaluate a manager's demonstrable ability to coach their people for advancement.

5. Do you have a mentor in the organization who can help you make contacts that you aren't able to make on your own?
A good mentor will also give you feedback and talk realistically about qualifications and what you might need to do to be promotable. Make sure you're clear with your mentor about what you're seeking from them.

6. Do you need to move on from this organization?
Sometimes a job elsewhere gives you a leg up. If you come back, you might be able to apply at a higher level.

7. Can you mentor those who come up behind you?
Generously share whatever wisdom you've gleaned about navigating the system.

◇◇

Summary for Dealing with Any Poor Me Jerk

- Be aware of your limitations to help people who are fearful. People who are phobic likely need more help than you can offer and might benefit from a referral to outside counseling resources.
- Set boundaries. If you're being asked to do their work because they're afraid, send them to your boss and stop doing their work. If your boss asks you to pick it up, see if you can negotiate compensation, trades, or opportunities such as a premium for taking on the additional assignment—although you may be told it falls under "other duties as assigned." In that case, be gracious and make note of your positive contribution to discuss at your next performance review.
- Listen well. The ability to summarize what a person has said is extremely valuable and may help them sort out what they really think or believe.
- Recognize your limits for listening to someone complain. When you've had enough, cut it off. How often this person comes to you will have to do with how willing you are to listen. If you don't know how to end a conversation, see the section on How to Deal with Dramatics and Non-Stop Talkers in the Narcissistic Jerk chapter.

- Guide them in the direction of becoming informed if they're willing. If you believe the person is missing information that would be helpful, ask if you might offer what you know or resources that could assist.
- Share your observations with them, if desired. If you have firsthand knowledge about behavior that gets in their way, ask if they want to hear it. If the answer is no, stop.
- Generously mentor others who desire career growth, if you're in a position to do so.

Chapter Eight:

THE JOKESTER JERK

Humor can be a wonderfully healing and bonding experience. Remember times when you and others have laughed so hard you were crying? Hilarity like this typically springs from shared experience taken to its extreme, or the recognition that we've all been in similarly absurd situations.

At work, we may truly enjoy the humor of our colleagues—or grit our teeth listening to what we consider lame and obnoxious attempts. It's hard to talk to someone about their witticisms if you're not a fan because for so many of us, our humor is part of who we are.

We don't want to eliminate all fun on the job—how horrible would that be? Just be mindful of how your words land. Amusing comments about the vagaries of work can break tension, make the intolerable bearable, and is often met with a gleeful response.

Although anyone's humor can fall flat or be offensive to someone, this chapter isn't about one-off occasions. Just as with the other jerks described in this book, we're looking at a pattern of behavior over time. However, I would argue that the most derogatory humor (e.g., "You're a guy, what are you doing in a skirt job?") or other blatant harassment require a swift, clear, negative statement.

In this chapter we'll cover strategies for dealing with the following:

- **The Punster Amongst Us** (using puns to excess)
- **The Tone-Deaf Humorist** (not reading the audience)
- **The Just Kidding** (trying to soften the blow?)
- **The I'm Going to Get Under Your Skin Teasing** (unsubtle barbs)

The Punster Amongst Us

There are people who think their contribution to a conversation is to chime in with puns. They deliver their line, e.g., "I think the dentists know the drill," derail the conversation, and then wait for a dog biscuit with an "aren't I clever?" look. Unless you have an appreciation for puns, it's irritating when this happens repeatedly in a day. No doubt you've already given the deadpan response of "very funny" or "ha-ha" in an attempt to end it without realizing the results you seek.

You may recognize punsters by the following:

- They have a compulsion to come up with something. Each time, they mentally leave the conversation to find a witticism. Not only do they disrupt the flow of the conversation, they lose the thread.
- They don't need much encouragement to keep going. Any attention seems to be enough, even negative comments.
- They can't wrap their heads around the fact that not everyone finds puns clever.
- They fail to realize the rare, well-placed pun will go a lot further with their audience than a constant stream of them.

171

Bo and His Boring Puns

Sofia came to me with an issue she considered trivial but highly annoying. Her colleague, Bo, was a punster. They couldn't have a conversation about work without him interrupting with, "Wait, wait, I've got it," then filling in with a pun related to something they were discussing. Not only did Sofia fail to appreciate the actual jokes, she was particularly irritated at sliding off track and taking time away from what she was trying to accomplish. If it happened once in a while, she could've ignored it. But the frequency was becoming unbearable.

Naturally, Sofia didn't want to be accused of being humorless. She wanted to maintain a good relationship with Bo, who she genuinely liked. I asked her how well keeping quiet was working—was she avoiding him yet? She admitted she was. I suggested it was time to let Bo know that she didn't appreciate his frequent punning and to please stop when he was around her.

A few weeks later, I saw Sofia at the coffee stand. She confessed that she wasn't sure she'd used the best words, but she snapped at Bo when he'd made one pun too many and barked, "Really, Bo?" When he asked, "Am I bothering you?" she realized she had her opportunity to address it. She said, "I really like you, but your constant punning is really irritating!" Bo apologized, saying he hadn't known and would tone it down. Since then he'd made a few quips, but Sofia said it wasn't frequent and she could live with it.

How to Deal with the Punster Amongst Us

- Don't make comments like "very funny" or "ha-ha" in return—it doesn't work. That's just enough attention to keep them going.
- Try direct feedback. Say something like, "I know you think puns are funny, but you take the conversation off course and that's disruptive," or "I find your puns distracting at times."

- Ask them to refrain from being so expressive. A response you might get if you ask them to stop is, "But that's how my mind works." You might encourage them to write down their witticisms to share with a more interested audience versus sharing them out loud. There are plenty of online forums for people who appreciate puns.
- Try something like, "You know, I just don't find puns funny." You may not have much luck changing their behavior in general, but you can probably get them to change when they're around you.

WORKSHEET:

IF YOU THINK YOU MAY BE

A PUNSTER AMONGST US

Please answer the following questions with a yes or no. For each yes answer, see the advice that follows the question.

1. Have you been unaware that not everyone loves puns?

Know your audience. If you find someone with whom you can have witty repartee, have at it! When others are observing, though, pay attention to when enough is enough. Their facial expressions will let you know (as well as the "ha-ha, as I was saying . . ." comments).

2. Do you think you show off your intelligence to your audience through puns?

Please be aware that this only works with those who are appreciative of your humor. If you get no response, or a bored response, they're *not* your tribe.

3. Have you been told that your repeated punning is really bothersome, not just mildly annoying?
If so, stop. Save your best material for those who enjoy it.

◇◇

The Tone-Deaf Humorist

We've explored other jerk types who suffer from a lack of self-awareness, and the Tone-Deaf Humorist fits right in. They don't read the context of their environment, or their audience. These are people who figure if *they* think it's funny, everyone will. Their intent isn't necessarily malicious, although it can be. They lack judgment about their venue and with whom they're speaking.

Ways you might recognize them:

- They tell jokes at work that make fun of a category of people (i.e., based on their religion, political affiliation, gender, race, age, culture, etc.). Or they make jokes of a sexual nature and don't notice they're being offensive. When they get no reaction, or a mediocre one, they may continue to be oblivious and say, "Isn't that funny?"
- Conversely, they may be well aware that they're offensive. Some consider it a badge of honor to declare their immunity to "political correctness." They may, or may not, hold a bias—their point is about not pandering to what they consider to be ridiculous social rules (which the rest of us would consider being polite).
- Or they're actually racist, sexist, homophobic, xenophobic, or (fill in the blank) and proclaim this through "humor." More about this in the I'm Going to Get Under Your Skin part of this chapter.

Jocular Joan

Binh came to ask me for help with one of his employees, Joan. He'd been the manager of the department for about three years, and he felt he had a pretty good grasp of the team dynamics. He noticed that Joan was frequently excluded from coffee breaks and lunches by her colleagues and suspected he knew why.

Joan kept up a running commentary about getting old and made jokes about the "ravages of age." She'd end each of her stand-up routines with a knowing look at her generational peers and say, "Isn't that right?" Her contemporaries held no fondness for Joan's references to bladders, insomnia, digestive ailments, arthritic knees, and hair that either was, or wasn't, where it was supposed to be.

Binh didn't know what to do. Joan was his mother's age, and he felt it would be disrespectful to talk with her about this. I asked what he wanted to accomplish. He said he wanted Joan to refrain from these comments with the hope that the rest of the group would include her in their informal gatherings. He thought it would help teamwork if there was more comradery.

I had two questions for Binh:

- Given that Joan had failed to recognize the clues that her humor wasn't appreciated, how would she ever become aware if he didn't say something?
- Once a staff member has earned a bad reputation, it can be hard to turn that around even if the person changes their ways. Did he think his team would notice differences and give Joan another chance?

Binh said he wasn't sure about how the staff would respond to a change in Joan. He decided he wanted more time to think about the situation before acting.

A month or so later, I ran into Binh, who told me a golden opportunity had presented itself. During a meeting between the two of them, Joan made another comment about her "advanced years." Binh screwed up his courage and said, "I've noticed how you talk about your age as if it diminishes you. Is that what you mean to do?" Joan confessed that she'd been worried about being seen as irrelevant at work, so her jokes were designed to "get it out there" before anyone else could. Binh shared his observation that her colleagues didn't seem to see the humor and he wondered if it was causing them to withdraw from her.

According to Binh, Joan left their meeting somber. Apparently, she thought a lot about what he said because she changed her demeanor at work. Binh reported that she started asking people more questions about themselves and stopped commenting so much about herself. Over a few weeks, the freeze from her colleagues began to thaw. Binh said he'd observed Joan happily chatting with a group of colleagues on their way to lunch.

How to Deal with the Tone-Deaf Humorist

- Let them know if they offend. You can even give them the benefit of the doubt by saying something like, "Joan, I'm sure you didn't mean to be hurtful, but that was a harsh comment about newcomers." Most will apologize and maybe even have a wake-up call.
- Be clear it's not okay. If they respond to a comment like the one above with something like, "Yep, that's exactly how I feel," say that you don't appreciate them sharing these sentiments at work.
- Speak up if it's more awkward for the target to say something. If someone who is not of the demeaned group speaks up, they may be heard. If a lone (fill in the blank) addresses it, they might be dismissed as "too sensitive." But it's particularly powerful to say

something when you aren't part of the group that's the butt of the joke.

- Apologize for them if necessary. If the Tone-Deaf Humorist misses the chance to make amends to someone who is offended, you can address the person yourself. "Joan missed the mark there. Sorry." Yes, Joan might glare at you, but that's okay.
- Speak to them in private. If you're a close confidant of the misguided humorist, consider having an off-line conversation about how humor functions (or doesn't) at work.
- Elevate the issue if needed. If the humor is nasty, it needs to be reported to management or human resources. See the I'm Going to Get Under Your Skin part of this chapter.

WORKSHEET:

IF YOU THINK YOU MAY BE

A TONE-DEAF HUMORIST

Please answer the following questions with yes or no. For each yes answer, see the advice that follows the question.

1. Do you use self-deprecating humor?
You may be diminishing yourself with it, and if you try to sweep others into your ranks, like Joan did, you're diminishing them as well. Most people aren't interested in being placed in a category that's denigrated by a joke.

2. Have social mores changed so that the type of humor you use, and that seems acceptable to you, is no longer relevant in the workplace?

Because standards of humor evolve over time, take note if your humor has become outmoded and offensive. For example, picking on categories of people isn't okay, so please evaluate the content of your joke before you say it. You can reference your own family or community instead of a group, e.g., "My Scottish family . . ." versus "You know the Scots . . ."

3. Is your goal to be provocative using humor?

Keep it out of the workplace. Don't go on the defense; apologize if you've offended a coworker.

4. Do you hold views of certain groups that put them in a "lesser-than-me" camp so you feel it's okay to make jokes about them?

Please refrain from making anyone at work the butt of a joke. You might be well advised to get to know people from the group you disparage. The results could be illuminating and potentially life-changing for you.

The Just Kidding

Saying "just kidding" at the end of a statement is an attempt to lessen the impact of what was said. You're still clearly meant to hear the message—but "oh, never mind!" A few reasons for using this phrase are:

- They said something snarky about you or someone else and then follow up with "just kidding" to indicate, "I said it, but you're supposed to think I didn't mean it so you won't get mad or think badly of me."
- They may use "just kidding" when there's a power or hierarchal difference and they're imparting serious information that the audience might not like. It's

designed to buffer reactions and avoid getting into trouble.

- They use it as a way of concluding self-deprecating remarks. They say something disparaging about themselves, then use the tagline as if they didn't really mean what they said. Makes you wonder about their self-esteem, doesn't it?
- They use it as a ham-handed way of saying, "I'm sorry."
- They're not aware of what they're saying; it's a habit.
- They use it in an attempt to cover up menacing comments. Some people would call this passive-aggressive.

Kid-You-Not Ken

I was at a birthday party when I ran into Melinda, who I'd known casually for a number of years. I'd heard she'd landed a new job as the vice president of operations at a social service agency. I asked how it was going—to which she replied, "Want to refill our glasses first?"

Melinda told me that she loved her work, her team, and the mission of the organization. But over the past two months, she'd increasingly felt like she'd bought a beautiful home only to find her next-door neighbor had an ankle-biting, yippy dog she didn't know about. I asked who the dog was, and she said, "Ken." It seemed that her peer vice president of finance had some issues.

On Melinda's first day of work, Ken came to her office and said, "You're probably one of those do-gooders who figures we've got a pot of gold stashed in the basement for you to spend. Just kidding! Welcome to the nut house." In meetings over the next weeks, Melinda observed that Ken frequently made pointed comments to others on the management team about spending funds, which he finished up with a smile and then said, "Just kidding."

A few days before, Ken had presented the monthly financials to the executive team. His final remark was to note that expenses exceeded budget thanks to operations. Without asking Melinda why this month was an exception, Ken turned to her and said, "I warned you we didn't have a pot of gold in the basement. The place doesn't run on unicorn farts, so I hope you've decided what services we'll be cutting." The collective silence was deafening. Ken offered his usual, "You know I'm just kidding, right?"

I asked Melinda how the president responded. She said that their conflict-averse president, Marie, looked stunned, said nothing to Ken, then moved on to the next agenda item. After the meeting, the vice president of information technology walked with Melinda back to her office, reassuring her that everyone had been in Ken's crosshairs at one time or another.

Melinda wanted to confront Ken and asked for my counsel. Should she say something to Marie too? I asked her why she thought Marie put up with Ken's behavior. What she'd heard was the previous VP of finance had mismanaged funds and the organization's future had been in question. Ken had a reputation for being tight with the bottom line and had been recruited by a board member who knew him. He reportedly took the position as a favor and suffered a pay cut. As promised, Ken turned around a floundering ship, for which he received lavish praise. Seemed to me that Marie was beholden to Ken and was in a difficult political situation with the board.

I asked Melinda what she planned to say to him. She wanted to set the expectation that if he had any problems with her or her team's performance, he'd come to her directly; no more gotcha's in public. I said her strategy sounded great except I wasn't sure he would play.

I suspected Ken had used these tactics in previous positions as a way to bludgeon peers into budget compliance. I suggested she also have a meeting with her boss, Marie, to clarify allowable expense variance. Then, if Melinda felt she had an opening, she could propose two recommendations. First, that the executive team agendas include discussion time for major items such as the budget. And second, if the executive team had never established norms, might a consultant work with them to do so? Melinda even had a couple of names to offer.

Melinda called a couple of weeks later to thank me. Not surprisingly, her conversation with Ken resulted in, "It's all in good fun, right?" to which she replied, "Not really. Please don't do that again." She had little hope he'd change, but at least she'd been clear. The meeting with Marie, on the other hand, went extremely well. Marie seemed relieved by the suggestion to bring in a consultant to help increase the effectiveness of the executive team meetings. Melinda felt optimistic about a productive path forward—and hoped that Marie would ask the consultant's advice regarding Ken's behavior.

How to Deal with a Just Kidding

- Confront it directly if the barb is aimed at you. "That didn't sound like kidding to me," or "That's hurtful," or "That sounds threatening," might do it. It's best to address this privately if you can.
- Speak up. A quick response to just kidding is, "Are you?" to which you're likely to get a "What?" response. Then you can bring attention to the habitual use of the phrase.
- Say something publicly in the moment if needed. You might try something like, "Let's talk about this off-line." That signals to everyone that you noticed—and you have the class not to confront them in public.
- Say, "That's serious, not funny," if it's about something that's clearly not humorous.
- Address the "never mind" aspect of just kidding directly if it happens a lot. You might try something like, "It sounds like when you want to take back what you said, you say, 'Just kidding.' Is that what you meant?" Or if it appears to be a veiled criticism, you might use

words like, "Did you mean what you said but hope 'just kidding' takes the sting out of it?"

- Ask if they're aware they say "just kidding" a lot if the phrase is used as a habitual tagline and you think the person doesn't hear what they're saying.
- Respond with an "ouch" or "yikes, don't beat up my friend like that!" if a nasty remark about themselves is followed by "just kidding."

<><><><><><><><><><><><><><><><><><><><><><><><><><><><><><><><><><><><><><>

WORKSHEET:

IF YOU THINK YOU MAY BE A JUST KIDDING

Please answer the following questions with a yes or no. For each yes answer, see the advice that follows the question.

1. Is something bugging you that you hope "just kidding" conveys?

If you think the phrase blunts a critical comment so the recipient thinks you didn't mean it, it doesn't. Instead of saying this: "Gee, is stinky tuna all you ever eat for lunch? Just kidding!" Say this instead: "I know you enjoy tuna sandwiches and don't mean to offend, but the strong odor is a problem for me."

2. Is there a reason you don't own up to your comments?

"Just kidding" is confusing. If there's a power differential and you want to make a point, there's a way of doing so without "just kidding." Try something like, "I'm not sure you want to hear this, but (this is what I think)." Or "Can I make an observation?" and then say what's on your mind.

3. Did you not mean what came out of your mouth?

If it wasn't what you meant, say, "Sorry, I didn't really mean that," not "Just kidding."

4. Do you make critical cracks about yourself and follow up with "just kidding"?

Remember that what you say to yourself is just as powerful as what others say to you—if not more so.

5. Is this a habit for you?

Practice saying what you have to say then stop before you get to "just kidding."

◇◇◇

The I'm Going to Get Under Your Skin Teasing

Teasing isn't always benign. Many of us have memories of being taunted as kids under the guise of teasing, often by our "loving" family. The motivations vary: to put us in our place, to get a rise out of us, to embarrass, to be mean, or to engage in a power play (e.g., a sibling who demonstrates that you can't control what they say).

Teasing is on a spectrum that includes practical jokes. The point of these antics is to get a reaction to something unexpected or absurd. The response prompted by encasing a colleague's furniture in bubble wrap tells you whether the prank was mean-spirited, hilarious, or somewhere in between.

The malicious end of the teasing spectrum is bullying. When someone uses pointed and cruel "humor" to wound, it's abuse. We know what can happen to kids who are ridiculed on social media or at school. At work, this type of harassment is designed to make someone miserable, drive them out, or both. It's all about power. Bullies are often clever enough to assess people's vulnerabilities and choose those that will hurt the most.

How you can recognize this type:

- They engage in teasing that goes beyond good-natured to really being a pill. Now it's about power.
- They're delighted to see you squirm, blush, cry, fume, yell, or give any type of reaction.
- They exhibit a bullying quality in how they treat others.
- They may feel completely justified in their behavior to get back at you for some perceived wrongdoing—and you're unaware of the offense.

Leslie and the Homer Simpson-Sound-Alike

Some people are gifted mimics, talented and funny. As with puns, this type of humor can be an acquired taste. It's one thing to use mimicry as a shared form of humor, it's another when it's designed to prompt an indignant reaction. The following story falls into the latter category and was relayed to me by a colleague.

Leslie's coworker Roger had a knack for cartoon character voices, especially Homer Simpson. He'd fall into those dulcet tones with ease. Leslie found it irritating at best, but when Roger started answering the departmental phone with "d'oh" and responding to Leslie's requests with "boring!" she became incensed. She repeatedly asked Roger to stop—which he took as a sign to ratchet it up. Leslie went to their manager and complained. The manager didn't think it was that big a deal and said something to Roger about "toning it down," but otherwise didn't pursue the matter.

The more outraged Leslie became, the more Roger acted like an annoying fourth grader. The escalation continued with Leslie complaining to anyone who would listen about Roger's lack of professionalism, her embarrassment about how other departments viewed them, and the lack of action on the part of her (apparently incompetent) manager. Roger meanwhile chortled with delight and continued to spout Homer-isms. When he started referring to Leslie as "stupid Flanders," she snapped. She took her case to employee relations to demand intervention. Roger agreed to behave more like the forty-five-year-old man he was, and the manager was warned to stay on top of it. At last report, Homer had left the building.

How to Deal with I'm Going to Get Under Your Skin Teasing

- Determine the seriousness of the offense. Unless it is truly damaging you or someone else, try to let it go or ignore it. What fun is it to continue if they can't get a rise out of you? Paying no attention could end the torment. Turn a deaf ear, walk away, or tell yourself, "That's just Roger."
- Be candid. If you believe this person doesn't mean you harm, but you find their teasing problematic, take a chance and let them know. You might say something like, "I'm sure you're not aware of how deeply this bothers me. Please stop."
- Confront the issue. If they know it's really bothering you but continue, you might ask, "Why do you do this?" If the answer is to get a reaction, then stop giving them what they want. If it's their misguided attempt to dull your sensitivities to what they're saying, let them know it's having the opposite effect.
- Report harassment. Go to your boss, union rep, or human resources.
- Be honest about the teasing's effect on you. Teasing comments may be a poorly executed attempt to flatter

you. Let them know if it's offensive. For example, "I'm sure you thought teasing was a way to compliment my weight loss, but it bothers me when you draw attention to my body."

- Don't let an offended reaction in response to your feedback worry you. That's not your problem.

∞∞∞∞∞∞∞∞∞∞∞∞∞∞∞∞∞∞∞∞∞∞∞∞∞∞∞∞∞∞∞∞∞∞∞∞∞∞

WORKSHEET:

IF YOU THINK YOU MAY BE A I'M GOING TO GET UNDER YOUR SKIN TEASING

Please answer the following questions with a yes or no. For each yes answer, see the advice that follows the question.

1. Do you use humor as a way to hurt, harass, or demean people as entertainment for yourself or others?
Please find less harmful ways to have fun at work. What you're doing may be contrary to the policies of your company, or even illegal.

2. Has the target of your humor been telling you to cease?
Please respect their wishes even if you think it's not a big deal. Clearly it is to them.

3. Do you use teasing as a way to get back at someone you believe has hurt or offended you?
Let them know directly what the problem is rather than through backhanded teasing. You run the risk that they'll miss your point altogether or become more committed to doing what *you* don't like as a way of getting back at you.

4. Is there a group of people with whom you have an issue (e.g., management) and you use teasing as a way to convey your upset?

You probably aren't getting your message across effectively and are harming your own reputation in the process. Say what you really mean to the appropriate audience (or person), or let it go.

5. Does your family or social group engage in this type of activity?

If so, it seems normal to you. Do it with them; don't do it at work.

6. Do you feel like you have no influence over what goes on at work, and that's why you tease?

Harassing behavior is typically seen as a way to grab power and oppress others. Look for ways to exert a healthy power at work through offering to do more in your department/ workplace or outside the job through volunteer or other contributions.

7. Are you aware that if your teasing becomes harassment (or even borders on it), it may be cause for disciplinary action or termination?

The policies of your company may be even more stringent than the law. There's one more reason to stop doing it.

8. Do you use teasing as a form of flattery?

It's probably not coming across that way. You're better off directly complimenting what you like (hint: body parts are *never* a good idea to mention).

Summary for Dealing with Any Jokester Jerk

- Be brave and say something. It's hard to give and receive negative feedback about humor because it's a representation of who we are. However, humor is designed to be amusing to the audience, not just to the person who's using it. If someone's misplaced attempts are bothering you, speak up and be clear. Subtleties such as a lackluster "ha-ha" usually aren't sufficient.
- Share your insights. If the person is clueless about what's appropriate workplace humor, clue them in. Not everyone was brought up with the same social or cultural norms or has worked in the same environment.
- Be mindful of your own demonstrations of humor and how they land for others. Stay up-to-date and adapt. What's considered funny changes over time.
- Report those who use purported humor to harass or demean.

Chapter Nine:

THE WE ARE FAMILY JERK

Workplaces are communities. It's where many people become friends, and maybe meet their future spouse. In small and family-owned businesses, relationships can get messy. But even in large organizations, navigating personal connections isn't always easy.

A number of years ago, Marcus Buckingham and Curt Coffman from the Gallup organization did a study about what makes a good place to work (*First Break All the Rules*). The result of this repeatedly validated and updated research includes the item, "I have a best friend at work." We're social beings, and it's a lot more fun to show up on the job when you look forward to seeing buddies. Yet people's expectations may run the gamut from having no other friends besides those at work to having all of one's friends outside of work.

For those who enjoy having close work comrades, it's fun until it's not. If things go south, the people who surround the battling colleagues are often subject to collateral damage. Even when relationships are stable, issues abound regarding how to interact with spouses who work in the same area, or what you can say to the boss's sibling.

I taught a four-part leadership series at a company in California. On the first day, I conducted the class like I normally would by trying to engage the audience through asking questions about their experience and how the material applied to them. To each query, there was silence. I waited. Crickets. I was dying up there—no one was talking. I called a break, and a kind soul approached me to ask if I wanted to get some water. While we walked down the hall, he proceeded to fill me in. "You seem like a nice person," he said, "and I can see you're trying to get us involved. What you don't realize is that the president's sister is in the class and so is the president's lover. No one is safe to speak—believe me, whatever's said here goes straight back to the president." Ah, got it. I could only imagine what it was like to work there.

If you're flummoxed by some of the relationships that exist in your workplace and they affect you in your job, here's some help. In the following pages, we'll cover these dynamics:

- **The Family Ties** (when colleagues are related)
- **The Looking for Love** (romance that doesn't last)
- **The Best Friends Forever—Until We're Not!** (friendships that fall into disarray)
- **The Teeny-Tiny Gene Pool** (small, close-knit communities)

The Family Ties

The very definition of a company town means that a large employer is pretty much the one and only. Entire families work there, often over generations. In larger communities, relatives may work at the same place, but usually in different departments. Most companies have a nepotism policy that prevents relatives from reporting to each other, since being impartial could be a problem. The fear is that family would be treated more generously.

I was employed in an organization where the occasional married couple worked together. Typically, one was the boss. Likely they met because of their common education and interests and worked together because of their built-in trust. This dynamic wasn't overly concerning unless a worker in the area had a problem with one member of the couple. For example, let's assume that Dr. Johnson is the top boss, and the spouse, Dr. Brown, is the manager. Worker Marcus isn't able to get the answers he needs from Dr. Johnson, so he goes to Dr. Brown to ask for intervention. Is that okay? He's following the chain of command, but he's also complaining about one spouse to the other.

A lot of issues can be avoided if family connections are acknowledged from the very beginning. Employees need a protocol regarding who to talk to about what—and reassurance that concerns will be heard without retaliation. Although this section describes literal family, the same dynamics can occur when best friends co-own a business and/or are both in the executive ranks.

Other issues that can crop up when relatives work together:

- They bring their relationship to work for good or ill. That can leave everyone else uncertain or missing information based on a shared history they don't have.
- Their dysfunctional family dynamics may be acted out at work.
- They may discuss work issues at home, causing staff to become suspicious about what's being revealed—particularly if one is the boss.
- They *may* share information hidden from everyone else in the department or company (i.e., premature tip-offs regarding upcoming changes to the extreme example of insider trading).

Time to Move On

I'd been meeting with a manager, Grant, who occasionally called to ask for guidance with his customers and boss. As far as I knew, he ran his area pretty well, although he wasn't a particularly sensitive communicator. When the department needed to hire another employee, Grant alerted his nephew, Josh, and encouraged him to apply. Josh was just out of college and eager for work experience. This went through the employment system when nepotism red flags should have been raised and flapping. But Josh was hired, and the results were exactly the opposite of the expected positive bias; there was negative bias.

Grant came to talk with me about problems he was having with Josh. Grant said Josh was mouthy and unwilling to do what was asked. He complained of Josh's unworkable ideas, and his truculence when they weren't accepted. I spoke with Grant about setting clear performance expectations for Josh so he understood priorities and work scope.

As often happens when you only hear one side of the story, Grant's complaints were only part of the problem. A completely demoralized Josh came to see me soon after. He complained that his ideas were never appreciated and that he was being treated more poorly than the rest of the staff. He'd come into the job eager to learn from his uncle but felt Grant only saw the five-year-old Josh who couldn't do anything right. He was told how, and when, to do even the most commonsense things. I asked Josh if he'd be willing to sit down with me and his uncle to talk it through.

Both of them were nervous at the start of the meeting. I said I knew they both wanted a productive work relationship and also to maintain their positive bond outside of work. Josh choked up and said the familial relationship had deteriorated too. At a family gathering the previous Sunday, Josh was crushed by what he felt was snubbing by Grant. He reported

192

that he saw Grant leave the room each time Josh came in, didn't speak with him, and left early. Grant countered by saying he thought Josh was avoiding him. He felt so awkward that he left because he didn't want to ruin anyone's evening. Neither of them had any fun that night.

They each saw the other as the jerk. Grant's perspective was that Josh was proposing ideas far too early in his tenure when he didn't have the basics down; his ideas weren't feasible. He believed Josh's sulkiness and combativeness were poisoning other staff members. For his part, Josh saw Grant as stuck in his ways and unable to consider solutions based on current practices. They held opposite views: Grant saw Josh as barely competent; Josh saw himself as more than competent and able to add value.

I had confidence we could work on turning around their poor communication and misaligned job expectations, but the added family ties made the situation very personal. Did they think things could get better, or was the relationship already too damaged? They said they wanted to try, with each agreeing to be more sympathetic to the other's point of view. Josh promised to be more mature in his reactions, and Grant agreed to comment on what Josh was doing well, not just what he wasn't.

Unfortunately, it didn't work out. After several months, Josh came by to say that work had become so intolerable he'd found another job. I wished him luck and privately thought that was the best outcome. It'd become clear to me that Grant had performance issues as a manager above and beyond hiring a relative. How he handled the Josh situation didn't sit well with his boss, and within the year, Grant had been let go.

How to Deal with Family Ties

Although the following advice is framed around actual family relationships, much of this can be applied to issues where the boss's best friend works in the department.

- Bring the issue forward. If you believe preferential treatment is consistently given to the boss's family member, mention it to human resources or your skip-level manager (boss's boss). Be prepared to discuss specific incidents of favoritism, not just a "feeling."
- Confront the combativeness. If family dysfunction shows up at work, someone needs to call it out. Fights, nasty comments, gossip, and "We aren't speaking," are no more tolerable between familial colleagues than any set of coworkers. If you have a decent relationship with one of the warring parties, you might mention that it's disruptive to others. Otherwise, let your manager know the ways in which the battle is impacting you or departmental work.
- Express your concerns. Family members typically have access to each other that other staff don't. As a result, there's a tendency to believe that they're talking about you when they're commuting together or at home. They probably aren't, but it's better to own up to your concern than to go down a path of speculation and gossip with coworkers.
- Beware the potential consequences of hiring family members in the same department. This can be problematic enough when they are colleagues, but it's particularly dangerous in a reporting relationship (and likely contrary to the company's policies).
- Be honest about the effects of familial relationships on you and your work. In a small family-run business with relatives working together, the non-family worker can feel awkward bringing up issues having to do with how the family interacts. If you have a good relationship with the boss, you might try giving feedback about how the dynamics are affecting your job performance. If that doesn't work, and it becomes intolerable, you may be faced with finding another job.

◇◇◇

WORKSHEET:

IF YOU THINK/KNOW YOU ARE IN FAMILY TIES

Please answer the following questions with a yes or no. For each yes answer, see the advice that follows the question.

1. Are you currently reporting to a relative, or does one of your relatives report to you?

If your workplace has nepotism policies, make sure you aren't violating them. Assuming it's okay, you're expected to treat each other as colleagues. This means that you behave with each other as you would with any other coworker, not better and not worse. If one of you has trouble separating out family and work roles, perhaps you shouldn't hold positions in the same department.

2. Do you struggle to handle performance feedback from a relative as if it were given by someone else (which also isn't easy)?

You can't afford to become your teenaged self who hated having your parent teach you to drive. Don't act out in anger if you're given direction and guidance by your manager who is also your relative.

3. Do you expect a lot of positive feedback from your relative?

If they're the manager and they're treating you as they do everyone else, they aren't going to praise you all the time. If you're the manager and you expect your relative to be your constant cheerleader (particularly when you could benefit from some solid feedback), that's also unrealistic.

4. If you're the manager, have you been told (or get the feeling) that staff members don't know how to respond to what may be perceived as preferential treatment between you and your relative?
Make sure they don't have anything real to complain about. If you give your family member a pass, you need to give others the same accord.

5. Are you in the uncomfortable position of being the non-relative who isn't sure how to talk about one to the other (like Marcus in the example at the beginning of this section)?
If you're aware there are family members reporting to each other and you're reporting to one of them, ask your boss how to address any issues that might come up about the other relative.

6. Are you unable to leave family drama at the door?
Please don't bring domestic issues to work and subject others to your family angst. If your relatives tend to have lots of ups and downs, and it affects your mood and relationship at work, employment together may not be such a great idea.

7. Do you work with your spouse?
The issue of what and who you talk about when you leave work is on people's minds. Reassure them that you have other things to talk about at home and on your commute. Hint: having boundaries around home/work discussions might be helpful to your marriage too.

8. Are you the owner of, or work for, your family's (or best friend's) business?
Others without this relationship often feel left out or second-class. Please apply performance standards equally to everyone, regardless of their family/friend affiliation. If your business is suffering from strained interpersonal dynamics due to these

relationships, please consider engaging a consultant or seeking counseling together.

<><><><><><><><><><><><><><><><><><><><><><><><><><><><><><><><><><><><><><><><>

The Looking for Love

My guess is that just about everyone has been attracted to, or had a romantic relationship with, someone at work (at least once). You have something in common, there's access, and you can get to know each other before dating. Sometimes these relationships become permanent, to the joy of all. But if there's a breakup, or lots of tumult? Aye, there's the rub.

We've all seen (and no doubt felt) the telltale signs of love gone wrong: red-rimmed eyes, depression, insomnia, loss of appetite, the whole shebang. It's terrible for the people going through it, and it's not so hot for their colleagues either. If the former lovebirds are in the same department, there's the problem of running into each other—or attempting to avoid the other. Bad behavior can occur in the form of pointed comments, flirting with others in plain sight, or delivering a box of the former beloved's belongings to their cube or the parking lot. As a coworker, you may be caught in the middle, asked to declare your loyalty. It's the pits.

But imploring people not to fall in love with anyone at work is like howling in the wind. As Shakespeare said in *The Two Gentlemen of Verona*, "As soon go kindle fire with snow, as seek to quench the fire of love with words."

Some of the complications of attraction at work:

- Your company's policies. Most organizations have rules prohibiting romantic relationships between senior and junior staff members.
- Policy and law. If the attraction is one-sided, what may be intended as flirting may be perceived as sexual harassment.

- Miscommunication. You may think you're giving obvious cues that your admirer's advances aren't reciprocated or welcome, but they can remain clueless and continue to pursue—which makes it awkward.
- A reputation for repeated infatuations. When serial daters repeatedly dip into the work pool, it usually doesn't go well if their dates know each other.
- Unrealistic and/or unreasonable expectations. The lovelorn may hope for more than colleagues are willing to give when there's a split, e.g., listening to their heartbreak or requests to spy on their ex and report back.
- Impacts on work. The broken-hearted may be woebegone for a while, and at that point nothing's right—including the job and their productivity.
- Acting out. Insecurities and jealousy may have one of the lovers pointing to colleagues as competition for their beloved's affections, even when that's not the case.

Desperately Seeking Cupid's Arrow

Melissa came to see me about one of her colleagues, Michael, who'd been through a rough time over the past eighteen months. It started with the discovery that his wife was having an affair. The marriage ended and the exes were granted joint custody of their two young children. Given his battered ego and parental duties, Michael hadn't been doing much beyond coming to work and going home. But recently his pleasant demeanor had returned, and he seemed to be doing well. What brought Melissa to me was her fear that Michael had developed a crush on her. I asked what led her to believe this was true.

A month before, there was a volunteer opportunity to represent the company at a community fair. Michael and Melissa were on the same shift, which happened to be at the end of the event. When they were finished with their duties, Michael suggested they go out for a drink, which she declined. Back at work, she noticed that Michael had started manufacturing reasons to be around her, was increasingly close physically, and began touching her arm in meetings. He'd casually mentioned that maybe they could get together for a movie, to which she was so flustered she mumbled a "not sure" and fled to her desk.

Melissa didn't think Michael was a jerk and was glad he wasn't depressed anymore and had interest in dating again— just not her! She didn't know what to say to him and was hoping against hope that if she provided zero encouragement, the whole thing would fade away.

Many of us feel awkward discouraging romantic overtures. I suggested that the next time Michael went fishing for a date, she could make it clear she wasn't interested. A short statement would do it, something like, "I don't date colleagues," "Sorry, I'm not available," or "I hope I haven't given mixed signals, but I'm not looking." She could also make it more difficult for him to be in close physical proximity. If he did touch her, she could move her arm and give a little head shake. The idea wasn't to blast the man, just give him a clearer heads-up to look elsewhere.

How to Deal with a Looking for Love

- Say no to inappropriate requests. Don't get involved in passing along messages or spying on a coworker's ex. Tell them you can't do their bidding if your friend makes any requests that make you uncomfortable. Time tends to heal most wounds from Cupid's arrow, but it can be pretty miserable initially.
- Suggest they seek outside help if your coworker/friend has repeated has romantic failures at work. It's one thing to go through this with your friend once, it's another thing to do this repeatedly. Serial broken

hearts are hard to bear. You might recommend they get help from a counselor—there's only so much a friend can do.

- Be kind but clear if you're not interested. If you're being approached as a potential romantic partner and you don't want to pursue this, being direct is likely to end it a lot faster than hoping they'll "get it." Some ideas are: "I'm not looking, but I hope you find someone compatible," "I'd like to maintain our friendship as it is," "I don't date coworkers."

- Alert your manager if avoidance or battles commence between exes and are causing problems for the team. Or if you've got a decent relationship with them, tell them to knock it off at work. If they need to, they can resume hostilities once they leave the premises.

- Be transparent if you've been accused of being The Other. You may not even be aware that theory is floating around unless someone clues you in. But if you're suddenly being treated poorly by one of the sweethearts, and it's someone who's been friendly in the past, that's an indicator. If you have confirmation that this notion exists, speak with the person directly and say you've heard a rumor and want to clear the air that you *aren't* after their beloved's affections And please don't tell me you are actually The Other because if you are, you've borrowed a world of hurt for as long as the three of you work together. Jealousy is lousy and toxic both inside and outside of work. Avoid it.

- Alert security *and* your manager immediately if anything seems dangerous between exes (e.g., stalking, threats, drive-bys, persistent emails, texts, or calls, etc.). If it's your friend who's being subjected to threats, have them talk to security and/or law enforcement immediately. If they're hesitant to go, accompany them.

- Suggest your friend find some other venues for meeting people. Remind them of how many things can go amiss when dating coworkers.

<><><><><><><><><><><><><><><><><><><><><><><><><><><><><><><><><><><><><><>

Worksheet:

If You Think You May Be a Looking for Love

Please answer the following questions with a yes or no. For each yes answer, see the advice that follows the question.

1. Are you seeking romantic attention from a colleague?
When the hormones are surging, it's hard to remember why this is potentially problematic. However, if the object of your affection isn't returning your interest, graciously let it go.

2. Are you engaged in tactics to avoid, battle, or spy on your ex-love?
This is dangerous and career limiting. If you can't put this affair behind you, it's time to think about changing jobs to create distance.

3. Are you ruminating at work about your heartbreak?
If you find yourself drifting off into depressing thoughts, it's time to set limits with yourself. You need to do your job; you don't want to lose it too. Stew on your own time, or better yet, do something fun after work. If you're having trouble getting past this, seek counseling.

4. Are you looking to blame a coworker as the reason for your breakup?
Even if there was an "other," by seeking them out you risk looking bitter and potentially acting in unflattering and

destructive ways. Get help from a counselor if you are having trouble letting it go and moving on.

5. Have you asked your colleagues to spy on, pass along gossip about, or in any other way intervene with your ex?
This amounts to asking them to choose sides. Be the mature person you are and don't put them in that position.

6. Are you posting your relationship status with a coworker on social media (regardless of whether it's wonderful or in the tank) and providing *way* too much information through text or photos?
Your employer and colleagues can view these just as easily as anyone else. Are you really comfortable with discussing the intimate details of your love life for all to see?

7. Are you looking around for another romantic relationship at work after just ending one?
Take some time to figure out what you've learned and what you'd do differently. And consider finding romance away from your place of employment.

8. Are you already seeing someone at work?
Talk with each other about the potential for job difficulties if things don't work out.

9. Do you feel you're in danger from an ex at work or home?
Immediately contact security (if you have it) and/or law enforcement. *Do not delay!*

<><><><><><><><><><><><><><><><><><><><><><><><><><><><><><><><><><><><><><>

THE WE ARE FAMILY JERK

The Best Friends Forever—Until We're Not!

Work friendships that crash and burn sometimes hurt as much as the end of a romantic relationship. Most of us expect our friendships to endure, although they can be tested: one gets a promotion that both applied for, the friendship between couples goes awry if one of the couples splits up, something happens at work to cause offense, something happens outside of work to create anger. People can behave immaturely when they're suffering—and colleagues notice.

Other things to be aware of:

- Emotional roller coasters. Depending on the people involved, some friends have volatile relationships with lots of ups and downs. One day they're besties; the next day they aren't talking with each other. It's a pain in the rear for their colleagues.
- The emotional maturity of the participants. The less mature, the more they try to draw coworkers into their battles.
- The impact on coworkers. Some détente must be found if ex-friends are going to continue working with each other. Don't make your colleagues suffer collateral damage.

Darla's Distress

Darla came to me with a problem that was outside of the workplace but was dramatically affecting her work life. She and her wife, Alexandra, thought they'd found a compatible couple for socializing: Darla's colleague Gen and Gen's husband, Adam. They liked the same kind of movies, enjoyed the same restaurants, and had similar interests in outdoor activities and sports. By all reports they'd become the best of friends and had taken weekend trips together. When Darla became pregnant, she and Alexandra asked Gen and Adam to be godparents. Then things turned ugly.

A national election was looming with its attendant debates and ceaseless media coverage. Darla and her wife were voters but not into volunteering for a campaign, nor did they enjoy discussing politics. Gen and Adam were volunteering for one of the candidates. They kept trying to recruit Darla and Alexandra to do the same. Meanwhile, Darla and Alexandra had purchased a fixer-upper house and were getting ready for the baby. They planned to vote for Gen and Adam's candidate, but given their priorities, they had no interest in doing anything more.

Gen and Adam saw Darla and Alexandra's nonparticipation as a betrayal of their friendship and abandonment of civic duty. The polls were close—what if the other candidate was elected? Wouldn't they feel terrible they hadn't done more? Tempers flared during one last, disastrous, dinner. The couples stopped getting together on the weekends, and the offer for godparenthood wasn't pursued.

Darla told me that she was hurt and disappointed that it had turned out this way, but she never expected their off-campus relationship to become an issue at work. She missed the friendship and daily check-ins but understood that this was how it needed to be. However, when she overheard Gen falsely reporting to their supervisor that Darla was taking shortcuts in her work, she became incensed.

Darla angrily confronted Gen about the lie. Gen denied it even though she'd been caught. Darla learned from another colleague that Gen had been gossiping about her among the staff. Darla would be going out on maternity leave soon and asked me if I thought she needed to find another job once the baby was born.

I asked Darla if she'd spoken to her supervisor about the situation and its impact on her work relationship with Gen. She hadn't because she was embarrassed. The only story that the supervisor had was Gen's. I encouraged her to have a conversation soon, stick to the facts, not go into the weeds of the story, and to not trash Gen.

I asked Darla what she wanted from her work relationship with Gen: to work together without drama. Sounded like a decent goal to me—did she feel she could talk with Gen about that, or did she want to have her supervisor present? She said she thought it might go better with her supervisor there.

Darla reported back that she'd spoken with her manager, who appreciated being given some context. The meeting of the three of them was awkward, but both agreed to their supervisor's requirement to leave drama at the door and stop fighting at work. So far, Darla and Gen had exchanged cordial greetings and were no longer avoiding each other.

In my opinion, it was just as well that Darla's maternity leave was coming up. Her focus was about to significantly change with a new baby, and Gen's ire was likely to dull as time went on and the election became history. Whether Darla needed a new job was yet to be determined, but I suspected the storm would be over by the time she returned to work.

How to Deal with a Best Friends Forever—Until We're Not!

- Limit the amount of time you're willing to talk about this. If it's a fairly close friend who wants you to hear them out, pay attention to their feelings (for example, "I'm sorry you're hurt"), but *do not* get into trashing the other person.

- Stop nasty references to the other person. You can say something like, "I really don't need to hear that," "They've always been pleasant to me," "I have no malice toward Darla," or "I know you're angry, but that isn't necessary." That should be enough to keep them from coming back for your sympathy.

- End the conversation if you have little interest in this drama. A monotone "hmm" and a change of subject might be enough to stop their desire to unload on you.
- Suggest they seek counseling support. If you're worried about how your friend is reacting to this relationship problem, or they aren't getting over it, you might recommend additional assistance.
- Make sure your manager is aware if your colleagues are threatening each other or doing dangerous things (at work or outside of work). Alert security and/or law enforcement if appropriate.

<><><><><><><><><><><><><><><><><><><><><><><><><><><><><><><><><><><><><>

WORKSHEET:

IF YOU THINK YOU MAY BE A BEST FRIENDS FOREVER—UNTIL WE'RE NOT!

Please answer the following questions with a yes or no. For each yes answer, see the advice that follows the question.

1. Have you recently "broken up" with a best friend at work? Are you spreading around your hurt feelings or anger?

Talk to friends outside of work or a counselor to get support. Don't expect your work buddies to be interested in hearing your side of the story—you put them in a difficult position if they work with both of you.

2. Are you unable to keep a poker (neutral) face around the person with whom you're having trouble?

If you still need to see each other regularly, aim to be as polite as you would be with a stranger. Glaring or sarcastic comments don't look good on you.

3. Do you work side by side with this person?

See if the two of you can agree to be civil with each other at work. Even if you've had a massive fight, decide to get along well enough to do the work and not to pull others into it.

4. Are you considering "get back" strategies?

Don't engage in vengeful activities such as trolling, gossiping, stalking, or any other dangerous action. These things only escalate the conflict and may, in fact, be illegal. If you're that upset, please see a counselor for coping tools and support.

<><><><><><><><><><><><><><><><><><><><><><><><><><><><><><><><><><><><><><><>

The Teeny-Tiny Gene Pool

Anyone who's ever lived in a small town is aware of the advantages and disadvantages of knowing everyone. When you live and work together, there's all sorts of bleed over from one area of your life to all areas: you may be married to your boss's ex or supervise your ex's new spouse, your sister may teach your manager's kids, one of your colleagues may have bought a car from your cousin, etc. Gossip is often the norm.

The upside of small communities is the support, shared identity, and how folks rally around each other in times of need. But when everyone goes to the same parties and grocery store, volunteers in the same places and worships in the same congregations, how do you avoid slop-over at work? Although much of this section addresses literally residing and working in a small town, the same dynamics apply to any defined community (i.e., religious or spiritual, identity-based, interest-based).

If you're successfully navigating a small community, you've already learned a number of important lessons:

- Everyone tends to know your business—and they have opinions about it.

- People may be judgmental, but they're also helpful. Folks rely on each other in ways they don't in a big city.
- It's hard (or impossible) to be anonymous.
- Finding new romantic interests can be tough.
- You don't know when you might need a favor, become neighbors—or have your kids marry and make you in-laws! Never say never.
- It's wise to ignore a certain amount of crap that comes your way. It's important to forget more than hold onto grudges; otherwise it causes more stress.

If your family has longevity in a small town, there's a lot of accumulated history. Remember that children aren't their parents, people do grow up and change, and we've all made mistakes. This applies to life in general as much as it applies to being at work.

Peter the Principled

I'd just finished a presentation at a conference for educators when I was approached by a man who introduced himself as Peter, the high school principal in a small rural town. Over coffee, Peter asked for my advice about a gnarly situation that had come up at school.

Peter had to expel a fifteen-year-old, Ethan, who'd brought a gun to school. The sheriff's department was called, and per the district policy, that was Ethan's last day. The problem was the kid was the son of one of the English teachers, Eliza, a thirty-year veteran who happened to have been Peter's mentor years ago when he was a new teacher. Things were already difficult at home for Eliza, and Peter felt terrible about the extra burden the expulsion would cause. The next closest high school was fifteen miles away, and it was only halfway through the school year. Transportation was one of many issues.

Five months before, Eliza's husband had been seriously injured in a work accident. He was at home, disabled, and in pain. They'd planned to retire in four years, but with her husband's work future and disability compensation uncertain, their plans were on hold. Peter could see how the family situation set Ethan up for a fall. As the last child at home with preoccupied parents, and a kid who'd always been prone to questionable peer influence, no one had time or energy to guide him.

The previous week, Peter had observed Eliza in the classroom as part of her annual teacher evaluation. What he saw was a tired, distracted instructor who wasn't on her game—or keeping the attention of the students. Not only did Peter feel bad about Ethan, he needed to give Eliza a poor performance review.

In this case, the situation was the "jerk." I asked Peter what he wanted to do. He knew he needed to talk with Eliza about the classroom observation he'd made but said he would offer to do a second one to give her another chance. His biggest question was what he might be able to do to help relieve Eliza's stress.

I suggested he talk with the district's human resources to see if Eliza met the requirements for the Family and Medical Leave Act or any leave provisions in the union contract. She might be able to take a bit of time off. I asked if there were services in the community that she could use to stretch their family budget. There were but they were places she'd volunteered, and she was proud. Since Peter and Eliza had a close relationship, I suggested he remind her that as much as she'd helped others, the community would be honored to assist her.

I applauded Peter for being such a compassionate friend to his mentor. The tables had turned, and now he was the one who could help her.

How to Deal with Being in a Teeny-Tiny Gene Pool

- Tell your best friends at work what's okay to pass along. If you're uncomfortable with the amount of personal information your colleagues know about you, tell your buddies what isn't okay to relay to others. Ask those who don't follow your wishes to please cease—and reconsider how much you share with them in the future.

- Try out the psychological concept of "compartmentalization." This is a useful technique if you find yourself hanging onto grudges and/or hurts from other parts of your life and it affects you at work. Separate work from home by choosing to ignore feelings or information that leads you to be upset on the job. It's even better if you can release yourself from these feelings altogether; a counselor might be able to help.

- Ask that any feuds between your families be put on hold when you're both at work. If you and your colleague need to keep your employment, know that fighting on the job (or avoiding each other) may lead to unhappy consequences.

- Keep confidences. If others share information with you, be mindful of gossip's effect since you know colleagues both as fellow employees as well as community members. It's best if you don't pass along secrets or negative stories from work, or while at work.

◇◇

WORKSHEET:

IF YOU ARE IN A TEENY-TINY GENE POOL

Please answer the following questions with a yes or no. For each yes answer, see the advice that follows the question.

1. Do people at work know more about you than they should, and you suspect leaks from your friends?

It's never fun to realize your confidences have been compromised. Even if you confront your friends, you may not get the whole story of what happened or who did it. This is your wake-up call to be more careful about with whom you place your trust.

If you believe gossip or speculation about private matters (for example, the status of your marriage, your gender identity, medical diagnoses or treatments) has led to any type of discrimination at work, please speak with your human resources department or union (if you have one). If any actual discrimination does occur, please contact the Equal Employment Opportunity Commission or an employment lawyer (make sure you find out how they charge for their services).

2. Do you hang on to grudges and/or hurts?

Feeding your grudges or hurts with negative thoughts or behaviors is like drinking poison and hoping the other person will die. If "compartmentalization" (mentioned above) doesn't work for you, please consider seeking a counselor to help you learn strategies that enable you to truly let the negative feelings go.

3. Do you feel like you're typecast at work based on who you were in high school?

Family and small towns seem to have long memories for unhappy or embarrassing events. Don't bring them up yourself and if someone else does, you can try responding with something like, "It's time to let that go," "That's ancient history," "Moving on . . . ," or some other words designed to end a bumpy trip down memory lane.

Remember that as you've changed over the years so have the other people. Be careful you aren't judging others based their past immature selves either.

4. Do you condemn the relatives of someone you dislike to a damaged relationship with you?

Remember they're different people and deserve your consideration as being separate individuals. Better yet, try not to have enemies.

5. Do you get into work gossip?

If you've been the object of gossip, you know how destructive it is for people to pass along stories. People who know how to listen *and* keep their mouths shut are invaluable in small communities—be one of them. That's how you demonstrate your trustworthiness.

〉〉

Summary for Dealing with Any We Are Family Jerk

- Be proactive. If you and a relative are working in the same department, have a conversation about how you'll interact on the job. Be sensitive to other people's concerns about how your familial relationship affects them.
- Get help. If you're worried about how to address issues

THE WE ARE FAMILY JERK

with a colleague who's related to the boss, ask for clarification about the chain of command. Seek assistance from human resources or the union, if needed.

- Beware the dangers of workplace romance. It's easier to talk sooner than later about how things could play out on the job. Consider how you'd remain work friends if you're no longer dating. Or what could happen if you get serious and then, heaven forbid, split up.
- Keep best-friend drama out of the workplace.
- Decide how much you will (or won't) be involved in someone else's angst about their problematic relationships. Don't take on the role of go-between.
- Set boundaries. A skillful balance between different parts of your life is necessary when living and working in a small community. You need to be able to work alongside *all* of your colleagues, regardless of your multifaceted relationships with them.

Chapter Ten:

THE HABITUALLY ANNOYING JERK

People *are* irritating, in life and on the job. We all have habits or personal characteristics that annoy others. This chapter contains a collection of low-level chronic frictions that impact the workday, although it's possible to ignore a lot of things. But for the issues that bother you so much you decide to do something, the following provides examples and advice. What many people do is engage coworkers in gossipy conversations about how awful someone's habit is. Then they engage in speculation about motives, etc., while never speaking with the person directly. Not only is this not helpful, it's often hurtful.

Maybe you're embarrassed or worried for someone because their actions keep them from being taken seriously. Maybe it's something they're doing/not doing that leads people to avoid or dismiss them. If that's the case, it's a favor to clue them in—to be brave and say something.

In this chapter we'll address some nettlesome habits and potential responses:

214

- **The Scent-sational** (a potpourri of smells)
- **The Presumptuous About Me and You!** (a panoply of assumptions)
- **The Things We Don't Need to Know or See** (social media and fashion at work)
- **The Suspicious Sounds** (things we don't need to hear)
- **The Stretching the Truth** (what won't help you)
- **The Rude** (lacking in basic workplace niceties)
- **The Tell Me Something** (vocal volumes run amok)

The Scent-sational
(and Cultural Differences Therein)

It's shocking now to think that when I joined the workforce, people could still smoke everywhere. I was among the polluters, blowing smoke to anyone attempting to breathe. Fortunately, there aren't too many US workplaces left that allow smoking, but if you work for one, be mindful of secondhand drift.

I don't know of any issue that causes more emotional turmoil, cultural misunderstanding, and anxiety, than odors. Most of the people I've counseled over the years would rather have an unanesthetized tooth extraction than to have to talk to someone about unpleasant smells. Working remotely definitely has its benefits in this case, and if you're a remote worker, you're given a pass on this section.

Body Odors

This is such a touchy subject. Like many of you, I've had experiences with eye-watering, unwashed bodies and clothes, as well as those swimming in perfumed scents that left me gasping. Neither extreme is pleasant, although the winner for most difficult to broach is the stinky body or clothes issue. If left unchecked, a person can become ostracized or the butt of jokes and ridicule. You get the benefit of my experience in how to approach this since I've made my own blunders along the way.

215

Smelly People and Clothing

We're in a multicultural workforce and there are differences about what's considered tolerable, or even pleasant, body odor. Given that each of us grew up with our own standards for what's normal, the best we can strive for is a happy medium.

In some industries, people are given specific guidance about an expected level of cleanliness and fragrance because of the work they do and/or the customers they serve (healthcare workers, for example). It's a lot easier to fall back on an employee manual that provides clarity, but a lot of places don't spell it out.

Unfortunately, we don't notice our own body odor as acutely as we do others'. How many times it's safe to wear clothes before they need to be laundered differs with the person and the fabric. Not everyone does the "sniff test" before wearing that shirt one more time—and fabric deodorizers only work for so long. There can also be a problem with a person's body chemistry (or what they eat) that leads to a pungent and unpleasant odor regardless of how frequently they bathe. What to do?

If you are the manager of this person and you're aware of the problem, it's time to say something. If they're new to the workforce, you might be the first person to talk with them about expectations for personal hygiene at work. You can be very gentle, but please step up. To do nothing leaves this person open to humiliation or worse, including sophomoric retaliation like a bar of soap or deodorant left anonymously at their workstation.

As a colleague, you can also help by being kind and clear. Sometimes it's more difficult to speak up when you're a close friend because you could feel inordinate embarrassment. Early in my career, I was the one who hesitated to mention it to a friend. When confronted with, "Why didn't you tell me?" the truth was I was too uncomfortable. Being chicken is not a good defense.

The basics for giving this type of feedback: be direct (without shaming) and refrain from veiled humor. Leave the person a way to save face. How would you want to be approached if it were you? Not knowing and offending people would be worse, right? It's time to buck up and speak up.

Here are some sentence starters:

- "You're probably not aware that the scent of your jacket/clothing is extremely strong."
- "This might not be easy to hear, but I think your deodorant has lost its power."
- "I'm not sure you're aware that your body odor is pronounced."
- "You may not have been given this guidance before, so I want to help by letting you know what the hygiene standards are."

Perfume Poison

When I was a consultant in my own practice, there was a situation that resolved quite badly. I was hired to facilitate a group that needed to come to agreement on a variety of issues. One of the members of the group had terrible allergies; another participant used a lot of perfume. When I say a lot, I mean it came in the door before her. The woman had been repeatedly asked by the allergic man to cease, but the perfume continued. I was in the uncomfortable position of having allergy man ask me, in front of the group, would I please address the overwhelming scent as he couldn't breathe?

I took a very matter-of-fact approach and asked the woman in question if she would mind washing off some of the fragrance. I realize now that I should have *never* said anything in front of the group. But my impromptu reasoning was that we were still at the beginning of the meeting so calling a break would be odd. Now I realize I should've called a break regardless of the timing to address the issue off-line. As it was, the confronted woman angrily rose from her seat and yelled, "You're asking me to change who I am!" She stormed out with an impotent me pleading, "Please don't do this." Guess whose contract ended with no future work from this particular client group? I may not have gotten a better reaction one-on-one, but at least her dignity would've remained intact.

When you regularly use perfume, over time you become inured to the fragrance and use more. For the past decade, I've noticed I can't be around strong cologne without ill effect; this is true for many people. Strong scents in public places are a real problem for those with asthma or other breathing issues, so please be mindful of your application of them. Other odors that don't necessarily dissipate with time include aftershave, perfumed hair products, and some body lotions.

I don't know how many can relate to the woman from the example above—the scent she used was her signature and too personal to be challenged. The guidance for everyone: if you must use a scent at work, only someone who is close enough to hug you should be able to smell it. Otherwise it's too much. As with dress or hygiene, some employers have policies about the use of fragrance, which is very helpful.

Because people are reluctant to confront the issue, they try to get the message across through a vaguely worded generic email blast to everyone—or by leaving an office door open. But alas, your meaning may not be received by those who need it. At one point in the past, I was wearing too much scent for a colleague with allergies. Rather than tell me, he put a "someone in the office is allergic to perfume" line into a document that I never read closely. When I finally learned of the problem and asked why he didn't speak up, he said he'd found this was the best approach. Well, since I didn't get the message, that's debatable. My guess is he didn't know what to say and was afraid of a negative reaction.

Remember, the offender isn't trying to be offensive or make you sick. You can be kind but clear. Here are some ideas of what you might try:

- "Sorry, I'm very sensitive to fragrances and have trouble being around them."
- "The perfume you're wearing reminds me of one I used to love. Unfortunately, I've become allergic to scents."
- "Is it possible to wear less, or no, fragrance when we meet? My allergies kick in and I get pretty miserable."
- "It seems a lot of us have trouble with fragrances these days. Can we agree not to wear them in the office?"

Of course, you can move seats or remote in to the meeting. However, if this is someone you're around a lot, you might want to own up. With as common an issue as this has become, I'd be surprised if you get the emotional reaction I received all those years ago.

Food Stinks

Oh, the joys of shared breakrooms. When the microwave is used for fish, popcorn, Brussels sprouts, or any other food with a pungent smell, it's not necessarily met with enthusiasm by anyone but the person anticipating a great lunch. The same goes for smelly food eaten at one's desk. If you share common space, the stink travels.

When my dad was a sixth grader, he was asked by a group of boys to join them in eating cloves of garlic. My dad was an odd kid who loved raw garlic, so he enthusiastically agreed—not realizing that the boys' motivation was to have the classroom evacuated. It was and they all got in trouble. It wasn't too hard to sniff out the miscreants. Food smells have been with us forever.

Classrooms and meeting rooms are a challenge. They're often used for potlucks, catered meals, or lunch meetings. As with my father's classroom, the lingering smells can be overwhelming. Folks stuff pizza cartons in the garbage cans and then depart, leaving the afternoon's meeting participants breathing through their mouths for the duration.

What's the wise colleague to do? Maybe one of these suggestions will help:

- Mention it if it really bothers you. Maybe you can agree to use the breakroom at different times.
- Consume particularly odiferous food where there's more air space (perhaps in the cafeteria, if you have one, or outside if the weather is nice) rather than at one's desk.
- Take a break and go somewhere else while the scent dissipates.
- Ask if your food smells are bothersome to others. It's not a bad idea to evaluate the odors you expose others to.
- Make agreements about how food cleanup is handled in meeting rooms.

A related issue is halitosis. I've never forgotten my ninth-grade geometry teacher bending over my shoulder daily with her onion breath. The remnant smells of what you ate or drank are spread around when you speak with your colleagues. Some of us have bad sinuses, suffer from gum or mouth problems, or take medications that cause bad breath. Yes, you can offer a breath mint. But you may need to be bolder and make a comment if it occurs frequently and they're unaware. Again, kind and clear are the guiding principles.

Some words that might help:

- "I know I've got coffee breath. Anyone else want a mint, or water, besides me?"

- "I'm wondering if you've been struggling with sinu issues. I've been there myself and appreciated a heads-up that my breath was sour."

Consider how you would feel if you learned you frequently offended people with your breath. Wouldn't you want to know?

The Presumptuous About Me and You

There are many decisions people make at work that they assume others will agree with or be happy to support. It's bonding when coworkers celebrate each other's major life events. But when requests are frequent (and seemingly endless) for financial contributions to baby or wedding gifts, graduation or retirement parties, not to mention someone's kid's cookie sale, it's tough. Not everyone has the interest or means to participate. The same goes for expectations that everyone can afford (or wants to attend) after-work functions.

Monetary donations should be always voluntary and in whatever amount the person offers. Some people have solved the office birthday situation by having the celebrant bring the treats for everyone.

There are other presumptuous behaviors that don't involve money:

- Having your sick, whiny, or bored kids frequently interrupt virtual meetings. Yes, sometimes kids have to stay home, the schools are out or having half-days—or childcare arrangements crap out and then it's an emergency. Just make sure they are occupied during important meeting times, or mute your microphone if they're likely to be interrupting.
- Being intrusive in someone's life, giving advice, expecting them to be your "rock," or any other way of presuming this person is closer to you than they really

are. Friendships are meant to be reciprocal, so if they aren't returning signs that your attention is desired, it's time to back off.

- Showing up sick to work. Hopefully, the pandemic has made a permanent change to this practice. This has been a pet peeve of mine because I've been the one to get the bug from patient zero too many times and observed work teams play "pass the illness" for months. If your employer is so draconian that employees have no sick days and you pay for the inconvenience of being ill, I understand you're afraid to lose wages. But unless you can keep from infecting others by remaining confined, working from afar, masking up, and/or religiously sanitizing everything you touch, please stay home and get well. Not everyone has a great immune system, and you have no idea of the effect you may have—not to mention you're likely to remain sick longer if you're at work. If it's the big day for a meeting or other event that can't be rescheduled, can you remote in? It's seductive to think you're that important, but ask others if you really need to be there and expose them to your cooties.

- Bringing in your pets without assurances that it's okay with your colleagues (assuming that your workplace allows them). The love you hold for your animal may not be universally shared by others who have allergies or are fearful. Working remotely definitely has its benefits when it comes to having your pets at work.

- Barking dogs (or other distracting animal or human behaviors) on virtual meetings or conference calls. Please mute yourself if your animal (or spouse) is making noise during a meeting or have them outside of your work area until the meeting is over. The noise you're accustomed to can be loud and obnoxious for others.

- Being a one-topic wonder. Unless you're speaking with a very good friend, most people don't care to hear every detail about your passion, whether it's a person, yourself, a sport, or anything else. Expanded conversational fodder would be welcome.
- Assuming that your new favorite whatever should be everyone's. You may've had an epiphany, but please refrain from trying to convert the rest of us. Not everybody is excited about crystal parties, wants to drink kombucha, or has a passion for Pilates. Live and let live, please.
- Presuming we all celebrate the same holidays, eat the same food, use the same type of medical care, vote the same way, or hold the same beliefs (among other things). When given a heads-up that you've made an inaccurate assumption, please pay attention and apologize if appropriate.
- Assuming everyone should tread lightly or adapt to you because you're overly sensitive, easily offended, or quick to react. Please manage your emotional state and seek help through counseling if needed.

The Things We Don't Need to Know or See

There's a distinct generational divide on what's shared publicly. Not surprisingly, older generations vote for sharing less. Two issues that show up in the workplace are social media and fashion.

Socially Awkward

Social media is ubiquitous, and most businesses rely on it for marketing and branding purposes. Work teams may use social media platforms for communication. Some, but not all, employers have policies about the use of business and personal social media when it involves colleagues. This section is about the use of personal social media accounts with your coworkers.

Inviting fellow employees to friend or follow you can lead to some very unfriendly interactions. Some examples: deciding to unfollow/unfriend someone, they find out, and now they're offended; discovering photos of a fun team gathering—to which you weren't invited and your feelings are hurt; people posting pictures of others without permission. And we don't need to see drunk or partially clothed photos of colleagues. Remember that what you put out there isn't private and is available for future viewing. Do you really want your next employer to see you in less than flattering situations or learn about your frequent difficult days?

Managers, regarding your personal social media accounts, *never* send friend requests to your staff members or accept theirs while they're working for you (and maybe for as long as you're working in the same organization). Many people (including managers) use unbelievably poor judgment about what they put online. You, dear manager, *cannot ever* post about what a lousy day you had at work, the person you'd like to fire, or how wasted you got. It's a small world, and you have no idea of who is linked to whom. If I were Queen of the Universe, I would ban personal social media among coworkers.

Fashionistas

Nothing screams "geezer" more than commentary on workplace dress, so I shall claim that exalted status with full recognition that there are generational differences about what's considered appropriate.

If you have a dress code at work, you have guidelines. Some job groups require standardized wear for comfort and safety; some have uniforms. Other industries don't care what you wear as long as you show up with something covering your body. If that's your place of business, you already know what's acceptable. However, most workplaces don't have very well-defined rules, yet they have standards that are largely left to interpretation. With some luck, your manager has discussed this with you. Remote workers may have different dress standards than those required in a physical location, but don't assume this without checking. What's acceptable attire is often dictated by your job, your customers, who you interact with on virtual meetings, and where you work.

I'm guessing most of us can agree that we're not excited to see butt cracks. If you have a job where you bend a lot or crawl around on the floor, you need to pay attention to coverage. Have a friend give you the red or green light as they watch you move. If hip-hugging fashion is au courant, your shirt needs to cover that area. If you have a friend who's unaware of the view everyone's getting, tip them off.

For those of you working from home, be aware of what the camera sees and reveals during your virtual meetings. It's one thing to put yourself together for the camera that views from the chest up when you're seated, but many people forget that when they stand up, we see it all. Depending upon the angle of your lens, even when you're seated we may be viewing that which you'd prefer remain private. It's worth taking a second to look at what the camera captures before you start your call. And learn from the unfortunate employee who took her laptop into the bathroom with her and placed it on the floor during a virtual meeting. Her colleagues were horrified that she didn't stop video and mute audio. So was she when she figured it out.

Here are some general guidelines:

- If you wear it to the beach, clubbing, the gym, or yoga, it's probably not work-worthy (unless you work in those industries). How informal you can be with your attire is dependent on your workplace. When in doubt, leave clothing items like DIY cut-off shorts and cut T's for your free time. Even if you work remotely, you may want to have a "Zoom shirt" or jacket for specific meetings.

- Underwear is a good thing, but please don't make it the centerpiece of your outfit.
- Unless it's a raincoat (and you wear something underneath it), avoid mostly transparent clothes.
- Acceptable cleavage tends to be generational, but at work err on the side of more covered than not. Again, notice what the camera is picking up when you're on virtual meetings.
- Midriff and stomach not visible, please. You may have belly ink or piercings that you want to show off—display them proudly on your own time.
- Maintain some leg coverage with shorts or skirt hemlines. Beware of shorts and short skirts riding up if you stand up during a virtual meeting. The camera shows all.
- Visible body art as your workplace/manager deems appropriate. Ditto for footwear (e.g., sandals and flip-flops may not be safe or acceptable where you work).

If you're bothered by the clothing someone else chooses to wear, I'd suggest you live and let live unless it's a violation of policy or putting someone in danger.

The Suspicious Sounds

Many people work in open concept workspaces where sound travels. No one living on the planet is immune from unbidden, undesirable body noises. The mature person pretends they didn't hear such. For those who habitually generate additional noises in the company of others, a gentle nudge may be needed to be more formal at work and not let it all "hang out," or to let them know that their noise is bothersome to you. Please note that although you may be alone in your home office, the microphone on your computer is adequate to broadcast these sounds during virtual meetings. Examples of irritating noises:

- Discretionary belching and other gaseous ailments
- Popping joints/cracking knuckles
- Gadgetry that transmits sound that's meant be heard privately (headphones, cell phones, hearing aids, pads, phone alerts, computers, etc.)
- Tuneless (or any) humming
- Habitual throat clearing and sniffling
- Lip smacking while eating
- Gum snapping (or perhaps, gum chewing at all)
- Clicking a pen
- Drumming fingers or tapping a pen on a table
- Rustling papers against the computer mike during virtual meetings, or other inadvertent noises

If the person seems unaware of what they're doing and you can't ignore it, you might offer a gentle suggestion with a tissue, lozenge, or recommendation of your favorite flatulence-reducing product. Sometimes a small hand movement and eyes to their hand can quell a pen-clicker, joint-popper, or finger-drummer. Or a more direct, "Please stop."

Gadgets that make noise need more direct intervention with the owner since the person is either unaware or so used to the sound that they tune it out. For example, a direct, "Could you please turn off the alerts on your personal phone; it really bothers me to hear the ding each time you receive a text," is likely to work better than waiting for them to "get it." If you're on regularly scheduled virtual meetings, make an agreement that everyone will turn off alert sounds on both computers and phones to avoid a constant stream of beeps and bells. Additionally, people are often unaware of how ar sound from their computer speakers carries, and those wearing headphones can be completely oblivious of the noise leaking out. Let them know if the sound is bothering you.

I'm not sure there's a subtle solution for those who didn't learn basic table manners and continue to smack their lips or chew with their mouth open. "Please chew with your mouth closed," would probably work.

The Stretching the Truth

It's a problem when people stretch the truth in the hope that everything will miraculously work out. I suspect folks think lying will deflect an unhappy interaction in the moment; however, they may be postponing an even worse interaction later when they're caught.

Below are specific examples and suggested remedies for the initiator or for the recipient.

Saying whatever you've promised is ready when it isn't.

For the initiator: Maybe you're embarrassed or ashamed to admit you're unprepared. Perhaps you're planning to stay up all night so you can deliver it, but there are so many things that can go wrong with this plan (heroic measures often don't work out). If you aren't ready, own up. Let others know you need help or an extension. If there's a date by which you can safely promise project completion, let them know. Apologize for disappointing your boss, clients, or colleagues.

For the recipient: If you've been disappointed more than once by the same person who hasn't delivered on time, consider involving them in setting the deadline (and negotiate if needed) at the very beginning of the next project. Then they have to live up to their own deadline, not just yours. Check in along the way to make sure they're on track with on-time completion. You may need to enlist your manager in this.

Saying yes when you don't mean it.
For the initiator: The definitions of yes range from "absolutely" to "not in your wildest dreams." When you say yes as a way to avoid disappointing someone in the moment (even when you know that the likelihood of your following through is slim), you've only delayed the inevitable. At some point you'll be caught and have to deal with the anger and disappointment of the person who thought they could count on you. If the yes is actually a "maybe," "no," or "unlikely," you'd be better off using the most precise word.

For the recipient: If you've experienced this pattern with someone you're counting on, address it head-on and let them know you'd much rather have an accurate answer than a hopeful one. If they really can't do whatever you're requesting, you have the opportunity to engage them in problem solving, make other plans, or get a referral to someone who can do the work.

Claiming you can do something you can't, or have experience when you don't, or possess a nonexistent degree or certification, or any other fabrication.
For the initiator: You may wish what you're claiming is true, but you know it isn't. This can come back to bite you hard, potentially costing you your reputation, job, or both. Don't do it. If you have done it, confess. Yes, you may lose your job. If you've been a valued employee in all other ways, it's possible that you can remedy the situation by obtaining the training or certification required. But if what you've lied about has put anyone at risk, you may well need to look for another job and forget about a positive recommendation. Please consider this an important life lesson and don't repeat it elsewhere.

For the recipient: If someone you know has claimed that which is not grounded in reality (and assuming this is a peer), you can either let natural consequences play out or mention it to them. If what they're claiming to have the expertise to do (without training or certification) is dangerous to others, illegal, or in any other way makes the company liable, elevate the deception to those with more authority.

The Rude

Some people missed the basics. The phrase "raised by wolves" comes to mind. This ranges from not using "please" and "thank you," being a boor, stealing food, or taking credit when none is due, among other things.

Examples:

- Manners: Even a dictator wannabe should use "please" when they bark at people and "thank you" when they receive whatever was demanded. For the rest of us, saying "please" and "thank you" should roll off the tongue naturally and frequently. If it doesn't, pay attention and practice. If you need to prompt someone, you might try the well-worn, "You're welcome."
- Stealing credit: Kids cheat on tests by copying their smarter or more studious classmate's work. The adult version of this illicit activity is taking credit when you're not entitled. There are ethical issues with this and certainly moral ones. Err on the side of publicly praising those who help you, the department, and/or the institution. If someone else's work is embedded in yours, give them credit after receiving permission to use their material. Managers, this applies to you too. Those who are in academia and science (among other fields) know that there are strict rules around the ethical use of research and other intellectual property, and what constitutes a violation. If someone is taking credit for your work, bring it up with those who can make a difference.

- Greetings: Surprisingly, some people don't say hello to their colleagues because the coworkers are lacking in hierarchical stature in comparison to theirs. At least that's how it comes across to those people who are left standing on the sidelines with a smile and ready greeting as a bigwig passes by. Minimally, you can smile and nod at people even if you don't manage to get words out. If your fear is that by being superficially polite, you'll be dragged into a conversation you don't have time to engage in, you can always keep walking as you say, "Sorry to be in such a rush." And if you're regularly subjected to the cold shoulder, you can try warming it up by saying hello anyway and not judge a lack of response. Just keep at it. My guess is you'll eventually get a hello back.

- Recognition: It's unsettling to be in repeated meetings with people and be met by a blank face rather than some acknowledgement. There is the neurological disorder of prosopagnosia which causes lack of facial recognition but that's 3 percent of the population. Even if you feel your social skills are somewhat spotty in the area of pleasantries, you might try giving people a nod when you see them. And if you're wondering why someone doesn't acknowledge you, then make the first move and say hello.

- Pilfering: Taking someone else's food from the breakroom refrigerator is never okay unless you've been given permission. If treats are left out for a work group and you're not part of that group, it's stealing plain and simple. If you're salivating, please ask before taking. If you know there's a frequent lifter of food, you can indicate you've noticed and ask them to please cease or ask for permission first.

The Tell Me Something—Vocal Volume Hurdles

Some people have extremely loud voices and laughs, and/or voices that would shatter glass because of the pitch. If you've been told to quiet down, you know who you are, so please pay attention to the volume of your voice. It's tiring for your colleagues to keep reminding you or stare you down over the cube wall or close the door to the conference room (or your office, if you're lucky enough to have one). Your vocal projection probably still carries through walls and doors. And it's the same issue during a virtual meeting if people are leaping to turn down the volume on their computers or asking you to lower your voice when you speak.

What you hear in your head is not what other people hear. It's possible you have a hearing issue. You may not think it's a big deal, but it can be really intrusive for your colleagues.

If you're stuck having to give feedback to the person who is interrupting your life with their booming voice, try the following:

- "Jason, please lower your voice. You're interrupting my call/concentration."
- "Jason, could you please decrease the volume on your microphone or speak more softly."
- "Jason, I don't like reminding you to quiet your voice, and I'm sure you don't like hearing it. Please find a way to remember."
- Get evidence. Try recording their voice on your phone from where you sit and play it back to them as concrete proof.
- Get a noise-canceling headset.
- Get away. Can you move? For those who work in a cube forest, it's hard to get distance, but a couple of cube-lengths might help.

- Get help. Ask your manager to deal with it (unless it's your manager, then try asking, or the recording method if they have any humor).

The opposite end of the spectrum is the person who is so quiet you can't hear them. You find yourself repeatedly asking, "Could you please speak up?" Their voice sounds louder in their head, and that, too, could be the result of a hearing issue. Or it may be a habit formed early in life, and so they don't have an internal sense of a normal voice volume. It's a gift to practice with them so they can play with vocal volume and hear what it sounds like. I was soft-spoken as a kid, so until I got used to it, using a normal voice volume sounded overly loud to me.

Other thoughts:

- Make sure that *you're* not the one with a hearing loss that thinks everyone is speaking more quietly than is reasonable. If it's just one person, then it's likely that person. If it's everyone? Well, that's what audiologists are for.
- You might ask if you can give them a thumbs-up when their voice volume is normal so they can become more aware.

With virtual meetings, voice volume can be a problem because of an insensitive microphone. If someone's voice is habitually soft even after moving closer to the computer, you might ask them to check the volume settings on their computer or that they use a headset.

◇◇

WORKSHEET:
IF YOU THINK YOU MAY BE SOME
FORM OF HABITUALLY ANNOYING

Please answer the following questions with a yes or no. For each yes answer, see the advice that follows the question.

1. Are you the boss?

Be aware that it's harder for your employees to approach you about a bad habit than it is for you to approach them or for them to approach a peer. Your hierarchical status puts them at a disadvantage. Even if asked directly, they may not tell you the truth.

If you've received hints that a certain behavior is problematic for others, it may have been understated. An anonymous evaluation of you as a manager may surface the issue, but that depends on so many factors, including how the questions are asked, whether it really feels anonymous (hint: in a small department, it won't), and whether people believe that telling the truth will make any difference. You can ask a peer manager for feedback, or someone outside of work. Whatever it is you're doing you probably demonstrate in other parts of your life as well.

2. Is your annoying habit one that multiple people have commented on over time?

If you refuse to change because you consider your habit a misbegotten distinction, I'd suggest that you're acting in (what some would call) a "passive-aggressive" manner. If you know you're bugging people and don't care (or worse yet, you *like* annoying others), that's antisocial. That doesn't win you friends, and no one's career is successful without help from others. Depending on the seriousness of your habit, peop. may avoid you. If you honestly forget and slip up repeatedly, then you need to find ways to remind yourself to stop until not doing it becomes the new habit. It's okay to ask for help.

3. Is what's acceptable at home different from what's acceptable at work and you don't make the switch?

Place a reminder where you'll see it before you go to work or when you get there or both. You can train yourself to be "situationally appropriate."

4. Are you so wedded to this habit that you've made it part of what defines you? Is it frightening to think about not having this habit in your life?

If you've pinned your identity on some action or activity that really irritates others, please consider counseling to help you reevaluate your beliefs about yourself and how you relate to others. You are so much more than any habit and deserve good work relationships.

〰〰〰〰〰〰〰〰〰〰〰〰〰〰〰〰〰〰〰〰〰〰〰〰〰〰

Summary for Dealing with Any Habitually Annoying Jerk

- Own up to your part of the problem. If the issue has been bothering you for a long time and you haven't done anything about it (or worse, have been gossiping about it), you've become complicit. Let it go or take steps to potentially make things better.
- Be specific about what's bugging you. Work on using words that describe the issue in nonjudgmental language.
- Be direct but kind. In giving feedback to someone, being kind and clear can go a long way. Apply the "How would I want to be told?" question to guide you.

- Suggest alternatives. If your person seems open to change but is mystified about what to do or how to behave differently, it would be helpful to give concrete, nonjudgmental suggestions.
- Escalate if necessary. If it's something that is dangerous or illegal, go to those with more authority.

Chapter Eleven:

WHEN THE JERK IS
A TOXIC WORK CULTURE

If you're feeling lousy at work and it's not solely an individual or small group feeding your malaise, it's possible the company's culture isn't compatible with your values. Entire books are written about dysfunctional organizations and what it takes to turn around a culture, so I won't go into depth here (please see the Additional Resources section for recommended reading). I'll provide a few examples of what toxicity can look like and thoughts about what you might do if this is your reality.

Work culture is simply defined as "the way we do things around here." People become acculturated if they want to be considered "one of us." These are unofficial company norms with which you comply. Most of the time, the requirements to fit in are fairly benign. I remember working with a client organization a number of years ago where the (all male) executives dressed indistinguishably in light blue button-down shirts and expensive sweaters. The mid-level managers of both sexes dressed in white shirts and black or navy suits. When I made (what I thought was) a humorous comment about the "dress code," I was greeted with a blank face. I explained what I'd observed, to which the mid-manager pointed to the *black shirt* under his black suit. Renegade.

Companies have a life cycle. The beginning phase is exciting, hair-raising, and often insecure financially. The mission is clear, people are there because of their expertise, and everyone helps form the basis of what's to come. As organizations mature, leadership needs change, the financial challenges are different, and the culture evolves. How the company is structured, the norms it creates, the compensation and reward systems, the leadership philosophy and practice, all shape the culture—for good or ill.

If you have tenure with an organization, you may feel sentimental about a past when things were smaller, more personal, and perhaps (in your view) more mission driven. That's a common response to company growth or acquisition. Even though you don't like the changes, it doesn't *necessarily* indicate organization dysfunction. However, if the changes offend your personal values, it will certainly feel poisonous to you. If you can no longer feel good about the company, your management, and/or your work there, then it's time to consider moving on. Insisting the culture revert to a former iteration to satisfy *you* is likely to fall on deaf ears and is probably a futile (if not career limiting) gesture. Know that having your values compromised and feeling like you were driven out is no less hurtful than the breakup of a personal relationship. All the same emotions may be at play: betrayal, anger, sorrow, disappointment about a future you thought you had together. Please allow yourself time to grieve and recover.

On the other hand, a truly toxic culture can develop at any time in the life cycle of a business. Senior leadership sets the stage; if the dynamics are rotten at the top, the trickle-down tends to stink too. Below are three examples of dysfunctional workplace cultures followed by actions you might consider you find yourself swimming in a cesspool.

Turf Wars

Some organizations pit their executives against each other to battle for resources. When leaders are set up to fight, a sense of "we're in this together" to help the company thrive can rapidly devolve into, "I'm looking out for my own."

Often the staff are mystified by how budgetary decisions are made. When you're on the losing side of dollars and leadership attention, it's easy to assume your contributions aren't valued. Alternatively, if you're on the winning side of growth and bucks, it's seductive to think you're better than the rest. Leaders can fan the flames of distrust between departments and divisions.

When the "losers" are those who provide the bulk of the customer service and support, carrying out the bones of the organization's mission (while understaffed and lacking resources), employees get discouraged and even bitter. I've worked with institutions where the staff were completely committed to their clients, students, patients, or customers even if they weren't happy with the organization's priorities. The stress showed even when they thought they were hiding it. Comments like, "We used to be able to do that, but we're short-staffed," are meant to clearly communicate, "Our management is stingy and doesn't care about us or the customer."

Alternatively, flat-out grabs for power encourage the leadership to fight for territory gain. This isn't to be confused with reorganization to align like-groups to foster efficiency and better communication. Instead, this resembles a Monopoly game drive to "take as many properties as you can." Employees become markers on the board, moved around by a throw of the dice, unsure of expectations in their new reporting structure— or when the next reorg will change everything again. Which relates to the following.

eople as Commodities

Staff members are terminated in unceremonious ways and escorted out of the building by security. People are fired en masse effective immediately—all during a virtual meeting. Employees are considered "warm bodies" that can be replaced at any time. The pay is lousy and conditions poor, but the brass gets big bucks, nice offices, and parking spaces.

It's no wonder people become calloused and angry. Sometimes the rank and file get back through unhealthy power plays (e.g., chew on their colleagues, trash-talk the company, send an exposé to a news outlet, etc.). In my experience, this is the most common culture malfunction, and it has endless variations. Each time I've been witness to or subjected to this dynamic, I've wondered, "Can't we do better than this?!"

When the cultural norm supports a management that demeans and vilifies people, it's swirling in troubled waters. Unfortunately, it doesn't take much to set a culture off course: just one new senior leader who treats people like crap starts (or exacerbates) the decay. At first it may be hard to believe it's happening, so you give the benefit of the doubt. But when one good person after another is raked over the coals and/ or punished yet expected to produce high-quality work and remain loyal, it's clear something's very wrong.

I've had middle managers tell me their primary role is "protecting my staff." From your senior leadership? That's not in the job description of a mid-manager. If this applies to you, it's a clue that your culture has lost regard for employees and their value. There's no safety, no one has your back, and there's little sense of belonging (you may feel inclusion among your immediate team, but that's it).

I consulted with an organization where stock delivery employees were fingered as the culprits in a case where the "wrong" supply was delivered during an emergency situation. Never mind that the person who placed the requisition was highly educated, paid at least twice as much, and had placed a faulty order—which was then delivered as requested. The highest levels jumped in. The middle manager was severely reprimanded, which flowed down to the staff. No investigation, no advocacy, no attempt to make it right. The employee response? To fight with each other because they had no power anywhere else. Now that's a toxic work culture.

Go Along to Get Along (and Keep Your Job)

People go "with the (effluent) flow" because the consequences they face by not doing so can be brutal. Those who point out obvious failures, shady work practices, or bias can be labeled troublemakers or worse. This can not only end a job but a career. I was consulting in one company when, over lunch, my contact said she'd filed a serious complaint with a federal watchdog agency. She thought she might be fired for it. When we walked back into the lobby, two security guards flanked her and whisked her away. I was given a new contact.

It's inconvenient when people raise objections to the majority opinion, particularly when the risk seems slight, the project is highly visible, and the costs are high. I'm sure you know the story of the 1986 *Challenger* explosion since the incident is part of school curriculum. To recap, two NASA engineers raised serious concerns about whether the O-rings would perform in subfreezing conditions. In the face of what must've been intense coercion, they capitulated. Unfortunately, the worst possible outcome occurred, and the shuttle exploded. Can you imagine having to live with that decision?

The pressure to conform is psychologically complex. During an era when the cockpit crew were too intimidated to speak up, a number of unchallenged pilots flew into mountain sides. New standards and training were designed to assure that fear of hierarchy wouldn't silence safety concerns. This philosophy was then adopted by hospital operating rooms and is

241

now widespread: if you see something that seems wrong, say it. No recriminations are made regardless of job title, and it works most of the time. However, we've all seen news reports of people who blow the whistle (sometimes repeatedly) about acts that are illegal or dangerous, yet no one listens and the whistleblower gets punished or ostracized. Speaking up for what's safe or right isn't as easy as it should be.

What If I'm in One of These Cultures or an Equally Bad One?

I've described three flavors from a large menu of dysfunctional cultures. If the company norms contradict your values (i.e., what you know to be right and fair), remaining can become a soul-sucking experience. Yet you have many factors to consider, some of which may preclude your immediate departure. The following are starter questions for you to ponder as you decide what you want to do.

Where do you have control?

Earlier in this chapter I mentioned mid-managers who feel their job is to protect their staff from upper management. If this applies to you, is there a way to create a healthier environment within your immediate group? You might also collaborate with other middle managers about how your departments can productively work together. You wouldn't be the first mid-management team to behave better than your bosses.

Regardless of your job title, exercise control where you can. If it's not at work, make sure you have hobbies, volunteering, or other places where your voice makes a difference. Remember, you're in charge of your attitude. Remind yourself of your reasons for working there. You can choose to arrive in a positive frame of mind and allow the nastiness to roll off.

Easy? Not at all. But it is possible. Find like-minded individuals, walk at lunch, meditate before/after work, release tense muscles, roll your shoulders, place stress-reducing photos where you'll see them and regularly update them. Put a rock (or some other talisman) in your pocket that feels good to the touch and reminds you to breathe and relax. Don't skip lunches. If you do, you'll be even more stressed and less efficient in the long run.

Can you avoid the worst of it? That might involve opting out of some meetings, skimming through certain emails, and getting off of distribution lists. If you only occasionally deal with the most odious aspects of your job, it might be more bearable.

What's your proximity to the rottenness?

If it's a few levels above you, you can probably do your job on most days without being burdened by the larger organizational drama. If you report to the center of rottenness, or your boss does and it spreads to you, that's a different story. You probably have to engage in ridiculous machinations just to do your job; political intrigue sucks up a stupid amount of time. Unless you're the type who enjoys the game, this type of stress can be damaging to your physical and mental health. Can you transfer to another part of the organization that isn't so screwy? If you have a number of years left to work, please consider getting a position elsewhere.

What's your overall career plan?

If this job is a stop on the way to bigger and brighter horizons, gain what you can from this experience and plan your departure. Can you transfer or use your knowledge of the field and contacts you've made to get a different position? Be careful not to throw people under the bus as you dash for the door—you never know who you'll work with in the future.

Bad workplaces (and bosses) serve as a model for what you *don't* want. That'll stick with you for the balance of your career. You'll be alert to similar dynamics in the future and either not take the job or bail out much sooner. When the opportunity is presented for you to shape the work culture, you won't replicate this misery.

Are you close to retirement?

They don't call them "golden handcuffs" for nothing. I understand how hard it is when you're bound by salary and benefits. Plus, the prospect of finding a new job after a certain age is daunting. If you've been waiting to hit a specific number to retire, perhaps you could reconsider. Talk to your financial advisor to see how much difference it would make to leave work earlier than you'd planned. Perhaps you don't need to work full-time. Consider all your alternatives for the years you want/need to earn income. The stress of working in a place that's abusive, or you hate, isn't adding to the quality of your life, or your longevity.

Does the culture promote that which is illegal or dangerous?

I shouldn't need to tell you that you don't want to be party to that. Report it or don't, but know it's time to get out.

I wish there were a magic wand to fix the ills of your workplace. If you're convinced you've done everything you can to make your situation better, you've given it time and it still isn't turning around, you have permission to leave the building!

Chapter Twelve:

TO SEE RESULTS, TAKE ACTION

In the previous chapter, you may have discovered that it's a toxic work culture that's the "jerk," not just a colleague. If that's the case, please review the questions at the end of that chapter as you consider your options. If dealing with a difficult coworker motivated you to pick up this book, I hope you've found useful advice. The next step is to act on guidance that feels right to you.

Set yourself up for success by taking small steps to make a positive difference. Consider everything an experiment. It's important to get started; you can make adjustments along the way. If you have a couple of situations you want to improve, start with the easiest one. For example, let's say you plan to ask a teammate to converse about something other than their complaints about the boss. It's possible you have multiple annoyances with this coworker, but begin with one issue. If you attempt to address a catalog of pent-up problems, you'll overwhelm them with criticism and that's likely to make the situation worse. One thing at a time with breathing space in between. You want to build a better relationship, not tank it. Often a positive shift with one issue will revise your opinion to the degree that you'll no longer focus on what you've considered irritating.

Give Yourself an Advantage

If you're incorporating a new skill (such as being more assertive), experiment with a friend or loved one first. That way you can practice in a less stressful situation than work. For example, to try out assertiveness you might declare where you'd like to go for dinner instead of asking others what they want to do. Baby steps. That doesn't mean you can't negotiate, but you want to make stating your preferences part of your repertoire. Or if you know someone who has some of the same characteristics as the person you're trying to influence, enlist their help. You can try out what you want to say on them to see how it lands.

Sometimes it's advisable to be transparent with your problem person about your motives. An example: If your colleague has expected you to do part of their work and your plan is to no longer perform their tasks, you can preview the future with something like, "I want to give you a heads-up that I won't be able to (fill in the blank) anymore. I have every confidence in your ability to do this on your own." If you get pushback, you can say, "I'm sorry, but that's my final answer." If your boss forgot they initially assigned the work to your colleague, you might want to remind them so they're not surprised by the change.

Then follow through. What happens if you relent and think, "Oh, just this once"? If you're on-again, off-again, they'll figure, "If I just push a little harder or ask later, they'll do it." Behaviorists call this intermittent reinforcement— sometimes the rat gets the kibble and sometimes it doesn't, so it presses the bar harder and faster.

What If You Get a Grumpy Response?

Not everyone will respond positively to feedback that requests they change. Actually, many people won't. Give them the grace to save face. That means they might bark, but don't let a snarky response deter you. What they say is less telling than what they do; the proof is in their actions. You might even get an apology later—but don't count on it. Similarly, don't believe an enthusiastic, "Sure, you bet!" without demonstration of change. When you do see an adjustment, though, acknowledge and praise. If you want something to continue, let them know you're pleased rather than giving a cranky response of, "About time."

If you've postponed bringing up an issue, their legitimate response could be, "So why is this a problem now?" or "Why didn't you tell me before?" You know why you've delayed, so own up and apologize. Some examples: "I'm sorry, I didn't know how to bring it up," "I apologize for not mentioning this sooner, I was embarrassed," "I regret not saying something earlier, but it's recently become too much," "I apologize for not speaking up until now, but it's built up over time." It's okay to reveal that you're not perfect either. The failure to address a long-standing issue means that *you* own part of the problem. Offering a further apology of, "I'm sorry for my part in this," may help.

Are You Willing to Allow This Person to Do Better?

As mentioned before, if you want somebody to maintain change, it's important to acknowledge and thank them for the effort. This is particularly true when the person has been a repeat offender; your annoyance makes it easy to be stingy with appreciation. Be on the alert to be pleasantly surprised. Otherwise, you'll sabotage your efforts because you won't be looking for the desired actions. Be that person who gives compliments, not just complaint or criticism. Look for what they're doing *right* and tell them you've noticed.

If you want to repair a relationship, finding real reasons to praise someone is one of the best ways. "Real" is meaningful to the person, specific, and incorporates detail. That means saying something beyond "good job." An example might be, "Thanks for bringing the meeting back to the agenda when we got off track. I appreciate it."

You don't have to like this person to notice they did something good. If you don't like them, it's even more important you look for what they do well and comment. Otherwise, you're likely to be biased to the negative (seeing what they don't do or what you don't like), which only reinforces your disparaging view.

What If You Get a Cynical Reaction from Colleagues?

If your group is jaded and tends to trash those who want to improve the workplace, you'll probably get grief for your positive steps. Continue anyway. Say something like, "I'm trying this out to see if it makes a difference," or "I'm tired of whining and doing nothing to make things better," or "Being cynical just depresses me." As things improve, you just might gain allies who are willing to help.

Is There Ever a Place for Documentation?

The simple answer is yes. If you've attempted to work out an issue on your own to no avail and the situation continues to be significant, you might want to keep note of what happened, the date(s), who was involved, and the names of any witnesses. It's a lot easier to present concerns to your boss, human resources, the union, etc. if you have the facts in black and white rather than having to rely on memory.

The caveat is that people who document every breath a colleague takes have their own problems. Don't be that person. If you're hyperalert to monitor transgressions by your nemesis, notice who's become difficult.

What If Nothing Seems to Be Working?

It's easy to become discouraged if you've given feedback or requested a change in behavior with your jerk and it didn't seem to matter. Or if you've spoken with your boss and you don't know if they did anything about it because you haven't seen change. Managers shouldn't talk to their staff about performance feedback they've given to others, so you're unlikely to be in the loop. You can mention it again but not daily (otherwise, you've become your boss's next problem).

It might take a while to notice improvements, especially with habits. It's also possible you'll see spotty performance (good one day, slipups another). You want to comment positively on *any* forward movement. Also, be aware that your message may need to be repeated for it to sink in. Giving a reminder is your aim—not being a pest.

If "success" to you means an apology should be offered along with behavior change, that's a tough standard. Don't expect an admission of wrongdoing or make that your goal.

How much you share with coworkers about what you're doing is up to you. Personally, I'd stay away from mentioning anything that could be turned into gossip or leave you feeling awkward or overly scrutinized. Feel free to share with friends and family outside of work so they can support you in your efforts.

Take satisfaction in your own actions because that's where you have control. One of the tenets of assertiveness is that it's defined by how you behave, not whether you got your way. Similarly, you may follow guidance from this book perfectly and not achieve your hoped-for results. If you've been assertive, set boundaries, given feedback, used stress reduction techniques, or changed your own thoughts and behavior— you've done your part, and you're entitled to feel great about that! You've also added to your skill set.

If there's no change and you're upset or angry, you have choices to make about your reaction. Do you want to continue to be ticked off or let it go? How much of your bandwidth are you willing to give this? You can try the mind diversion strategies discussed in previous chapters to make your circumstances more tolerable (for example, change what you say to yourself or look for a color in your environment to distract you). Find what you can appreciate about the person even if there's a behavior that drives you a bit crackers.

If the situation has become truly untenable, then maybe it's time to get out. If your company is large enough, you might find assistance through human resources, or you may want to speak with a career counselor about finding your next job.

Make It Intentional

I believe in setting intentions. For over a decade, my practice has been to write intentions each day. That way I'm priming my brain to focus and be on alert for opportunities. I don't limit my intentions to a to-do list. I add in quality and attitude as well. One intention I set on days I drive is, "I intend to be safe and on time everywhere I go." Amazing how often I end up saying that aloud in the car as I choose to stop at a yellow light versus speeding through as it's turning red. I also declare to myself how I want to show up at work. For example, a statement like, "Today I intend to be an excellent coach for my clients," focuses me on listening well and asking relevant questions before offering suggestions. I think the act of writing intentions adds power to what your subconscious receives since the message comes via fingers, eyes, and sub-vocalization. But saying them aloud works too. Regular practice is more important than the format.

Finally . . .

The longer I've been in the workforce, the more philosophical I've become about working with others. I attribute this to awareness of behavior patterns (Jerketypes) and noticing that other people's actions (usually) aren't aimed at me personally. The list of what bugs me has remained fairly consistent over my career. My understanding of what I can or can't do about someone else has become clearer. I take responsibility for what's mine to do to make a positive difference and attempt to let the rest go. Yet I still have my moments because, like everyone else, I'm still growing.

We probably have the most to learn about ourselves through the difficult relationships in our lives. You don't have to spend all your time there—in fact, I'd advise taking frequent and enjoyable respites to be with those you find compatible. But don't be afraid to engage with your more problematic associates either.

Please know that I'm wishing you all the best as you work through boss or colleague issues that have been difficult. Remember that the only person you can change is you and what you say and do really does affect others. If you're more content, you'll influence others to be so too. And that's a win-win. It's my fondest hope that you'll be happier in your job!

ADDITIONAL RESOURCES

Some of my favorite books were published a while ago, but interpersonal skills don't go out of date.

For Communication Skills:

Patterson, Kerry, Jospeh Grenny, Ron McMillan, and Al Switzler. *Crucial Conversations: Tools for Talking When Stakes Are High.* 2nd ed. New York, NY: McGraw-Hill, 2011.

The language used in this book provides easy-to-understand concepts, examples, and help for how to productively engage in difficult conversations and give critical feedback. There are other books by the authors, but I like this one in particular.

For Self-Awareness:

Goleman, Daniel. *Working with Emotional Intelligence.* New York, NY: Bantam Books, 2006.

Goleman, Daniel, Richard Boyatzis, and Annie McKee. *Primal Leadership: Unleashing the Power of Emotional Intelligence.* Boston, MA: Harvard Business School Press, 2013.

There are a lot of books out on emotional intelligence (EI or EQ), but Goleman was one of the first to explore this topic. *Working with Emotional Intelligence* is for everyone, although occasionally there's a slant toward assuming one has management authority. *Primal Leadership* is about leading with emotional intelligence (which anyone can use regardless of their position!). There are wonderful descriptions in the appendix that provide definitions of emotional intelligence categories and what comprises each.

For Conflict Management:

Fisher, Roger, William Ury, and Bruce Patton. *Getting to Yes: Negotiating Agreement without Giving In.* 3rd ed. New York, NY: Penguin Publishing Group, 2011.

This book initiated my love for the Harvard Negotiation Project. The first book was published in 1990, but the authors have continued to revise (with Patton stepping in after Fisher passed away). It is the blueprint for win-win negotiation and has been used in international conflict situations as well as daily life. The authors provide excellent examples in the revised editions about how to stay true to one's principles, even in the face of those who behave poorly. There's virtually nothing from this group that I wouldn't recommend. See *Difficult Conversations* below.

Stone, Douglas, Sheila Heen, and Bruce Patton. *Difficult Conversations: How to Discuss What Matters Most.* New York, NY: Penguin Books, 2010.

This book is filled with examples and practical ways to handle confrontation. Their approach may really resonate for those who appreciate more analytical strategies.

For Workplace Culture:

Coyle, Daniel. *The Culture Code: The Secrets of Highly Successful Groups.* New York, NY: Bantam Books, 2018.

I love this book! It's about what constitutes a good culture and the practices that will get you there. Coyle draws his

examples from a variety of industries (including the improvisa-
tional theater company Upright Citizens Brigade, which warms
my improv heart). He hits all the notes that I think are important in a functional culture, as well as showing us the contrast
of toxic ones. I especially like his chapter "Building Safety."

For Generations at Work:
"Generations" is an interesting concept because the distinctions between groups of people by age are driven by marketers
who target specific audiences. You'll find agreed upon start/
end dates for generations, but also variation. The current generations in the workforce are traditionalists (most of whom
have already retired), baby boomers (many of whom have
retired), Gen X, millennials, and Gen Z.

My counsel is to do a YouTube search for current videos,
then watch a number of them. The descriptions of the various
generations differ to some degree, depending on the age of the
person who is providing the information. They often focus
on comfort with technology and differences in communication methods (extremely helpful). What we do know about
generational differences is that each "cohort" (a group of
similar age, spanning approximately fifteen to twenty years) is
different due to when they grew up, the child-rearing practices
of the time, and significant events that occurred during their
youth. From this information, a profile is derived regarding
common values, perspective, and life and work styles. Of
course, where someone grows up impacts this as well.

Although generalizations about a generation may be
useful, remember that any one person may be quite different
from the stereotype. It's always a good practice to treat people
as individuals regardless of what you believe you know about
the person's generation.

To Find Counseling Resources:

Start by looking for what your employer provides. If your company is large enough, you may have a free employee assistance program (EAP). These services are often outsourced, which means your anonymity is assured because the counselors aren't employees of your company. Typically, a certain number of free counseling sessions are provided, and they can refer you to other resources as well.

Look at what your insurance covers and examine your benefits. Depending on your plan, they may list counselors in your area that accept your insurance.

Check out community resources. Most large (and even smaller) communities have free or sliding scale counseling options. You may need to use search terms like "counseling," "mental health," or "therapy" to find what you're looking for. There are even online services.

How to Conduct Behavior-Based Employment Interviews:

More Than a Gut Feeling by Richard Deems may have been the first on this topic. To find more recent material, search for "behavior-based employment interviews" or "competency-based interviews." You can find videos on behavioral interviewing, but many of them are about how to answer the questions, not how to write them. Make sure you scan thoroughly to find what you want.

Who to Contact If You Have Concerns about Harassment, Bias, or Discrimination:

It's probably best to start with your human resources department or union (unless they're the problem, or you don't trust them). To find an Equal Employment Opportunity Commission office in your area, look at their website, www.eeoc.gov/field-office.

If you have a legal department that responds to employee complaints, speak with them. Talk with the Ombuds Office if you have one (most universities and colleges do, as well as some other organizations).

Employment lawyers also answer questions about workplace discrimination. Make sure you understand how they charge for their advice and services.

ACKNOWLEDGMENTS

Although I'm not unique in saying so, every book owes its life to an extraordinary number of people.

Thanks to those with whom I had the pleasure of working and who trusted me with their stories. You inspired this book.

It was blind luck to stumble into the Chrysalis Women's Writers at Clackamas Community College! Thank you so much for your critique and comments—and your unflagging confidence in me and *Work Jerks*. I'm a far better writer as a result of being around you.

To the beta readers who read all or parts of the book, thank you! You were terrific to give of your time and feedback. Thank you to Putnam Barber, Susan Christofferson, Michele Coyle, Carrie Danielson, Anne Dwire, Barbara Froman, Denise Frost, Sue Hennessy, Mitch Hunter, Dave Hurley, Jim Jorgenson, Connie Leonard, Pat Lichen, Terry Liddell, Gordy Linse, Val Lynch, Kerry McMillen, Christy Miller, Laurie Miyauchi, Lisa Nowak, Shawn O'Day, Anne Reid, Lee Strucker, Debbie Ward, and Kati Weiler.

To my editor, Barbara Mulvey Little, thank you so much for your skilled ministrations to the manuscript and your unwavering conviction of its worthiness.

Bonnie Pasek, you were there for my fledging attempts in 2013 and I thank you for your encouragement when I picked it up again. Your design of my website is wonderful, thank you!

I could not have landed in better hands than those of She Writes Press. Thank you to Brooke Warner, Shannon Green, and the rest of the hardworking production team. I appreciate your help throughout the process; you are skilled and patient. You are wonderful advocates for women authors.

Krista Soukup, Blue Cottage Agency, you are a terrific partner in my marketing and publicity efforts. You're warm, expert, and enthusiastic about the book and me. Thank you so much. The stars were aligned perfectly when I was introduced to you!

To my dear friends who heard more than they ever wanted to about this adventure, your support meant the world to me. You know who you are!

To the West Linn Public Library where I wrote much of the second half of the book, I so appreciate the beautiful space you create.

And finally, to my feline writing companions Sammy and Davey, you kept it light by walking on the keyboard, rubbing against the screen, and letting me know when it was time to get up and attend to you.

ABOUT THE AUTHOR

For over forty years Louise Carnachan has worked as a trainer and organization development consultant helping thousands of leaders and staff members achieve interpersonal success in challenging work relationships. With approximately half of her career as an employee, Louise has firsthand knowledge about the complexities of navigating difficult situations while keeping the job.

Louise has worked in manufacturing, education, health care, and scientific organizations, most recently Fred Hutchinson Cancer Research Center in Seattle. As a consultant, her clients included various Head Start programs, Pacific NW Fertility, Bastyr University and Clinic, VA Puget Sound Health Care, a variety of Washington state departments, McDonald's Corporation, Starbucks, University of Washington Medical Center, and the Port of Seattle. She was also adjunct faculty at Seattle Pacific

University and Seattle Community College, and taught a course for the University of Washington's MBA program.

As a founding member of Seattle's Off Limits Improv Theater, for many years Louise could be found onstage playing any number of difficult characters (as well as inanimate objects).

Louise coaches select leadership clients and writes a workplace advice blog found on her website, www.louisecarnachan.com. She moved to a suburb of Portland, Oregon, in 2018 and enjoys her new state's offerings such as Powell's Books, Annie Bloom's Books, coastal towns, and her local library where she can be found browsing the mystery section.

Louise has a bachelor of arts in psychology from Scripps College and a master's of social work from the University of Washington.

Author photo © Kerri Ann Garfield Photography

SELECTED TITLES FROM SHE WRITES PRESS

She Writes Press is an independent publishing
company founded to serve women writers everywhere.
Visit us at www.shewritespress.com.

Lead: How Women in Charge Claim Their Authority by Ellen
Snee EdD. $16.95, 978-1-64742-070-3. Too often, literature on
leadership is designed for men—or insists that women have to be
more like their male counterparts in order to succeed in business.
Here, executive coach and former Catholic nun Ellen Snee shares
how women can find confidence in their own competence,
capitalize on their inherent strengths, and start leading in the most
effective way possible: from the inside out.

*The Clarity Effect: How Being More Present Can Transform Your
Work and Life* by Sarah Harvey Yao. $16.95, 978-1-63152-958-0.
A practical, strategy-filled guide for stressed professionals looking
for clarity, strength, and joy in their work and home lives.

*The Way of the Mysterial Woman: Upgrading How You Live,
Love, and Lead* by Suzanne Anderson, MA and Susan Cannon,
PhD. $24.95, 978-1-63152-081-5. A revolutionary yet practical
road map for upgrading your life, work, and relationships that
reveals how your choice to transform is part of an astonishing
future trend.

Drop In: Lead with Deeper Presence and Courage by Sara Harvey
Yao. $14.95, 978-1-63152-161-4. A compelling explanation
about why being present is so challenging and how leaders can
access clarity, connection, and courage in the midst of their chaotic
lives, inside and outside of work.

*People Leadership: 30 Proven Strategies to Ensure Your Team's
Success* by Gina Folk. $24.95, 978-1-63152-915-3. Longtime
manager Gina Folk provides thirty effective ways for any individual managing or supervising others to reignite their team and
become a successful—and beloved—people leader.